THE RISE OF LEGENDS
TO THE MOON AND BEYOND

by LINKED IN AND TOWN HALL ACHIEVER OF THE YEAR
EY NOMINEE ENTREPRENEUR OF THE YEAR
GRAND HOMAGE LYS DIVERSITY
WORLD TOP100 DOCTORS

Dr BAK NGUYEN, DMD

&

by 9-10 years old
WILLIAM BAK

TO ALL THE PARENTS WHO BELIEVE IN THEIR CHILDREN
AND WHO TRUST THEM ENOUGH TO LET THEM BE
by Dr. BAK NGUYEN & WILLIAM BAK

Copyright © 2022 Dr. BAK NGUYEN

All rights reserved.

ISBN: 978-1-989536-88-9

Published by: Dr. BAK PUBLISHING COMPANY
Dr.BAK 0110

DISCLAIMER

« The general information, opinions and advice contained in this medium and/or the books, audiobooks, podcasts and publications on Dr. Bak Nguyen's and William Bak (legal name Dr. Ba Khoa Nguyen and William Bak Nguyen) and his collaborators website or social media (hereinafter the "Opinions") present general information on various topics. The Opinions are intended for informational purposes only.

No information contained in the Opinions is a substitute for an expert, consultation, advice, diagnosis or professional treatment. No information contained in the Opinions is a substitute for professional advice and should not be construed as consultation or advice.

Nothing in the Opinions should be construed as professional advice related to the practice of dentistry, medical advice or any other form of advice, including legal or financial advice, professional opinion, care or diagnosis, but strictly as general information. All information from the Opinions is for informational purposes only.

Any user who disagrees with the terms of this Disclaimer should immediately cease using or referring to the Opinions. Any action by the user in connection with the information contained in the Opinions is solely at the user's discretion.

The general information contained in the Opinions is provided "as is" and without warranty of any kind, either expressed or implied. Dr. Bak Nguyen and his collaborators (legal name Dr. Ba Khoa Nguyen and William Bak Nguyen) makes every effort to ensure that the information is complete and accurate. However, there is no guarantee that the general information contained in the Opinions is always available, truthful, complete, up-to-date or relevant.

The Opinions expressed by Dr. Bak Nguyen (legal name Dr. Ba Khoa Nguyen) and his collaborators (William Bak Nguyen) are personal and expressed in his own name and do not reflect the opinions of his companies, partners and other affiliates.

Dr. Bak Nguyen (legal name Dr. Ba Khoa Nguyen) and his collaborators (William Bak Nguyen) also disclaims any responsibility for the content of any hyperlinks included in the Opinions.

Always seek the advice of your expert advisors, physicians or other qualified professionals with any questions you may have regarding your condition. Never disregard professional advice or delay in seeking it because of something you have read, seen or heard in the Opinions. »

ABOUT THE AUTHORS

From Canada, **Dr. BAK NGUYEN**, Nominee Ernst and Young Entrepreneur of the year, Grand Homage Lys DIVERSITY, LinkedIn & TownHall Achiever of the year and TOP 100 Doctors 2021. Dr. Bak is a cosmetic dentist, CEO and founder of Mdex & Co. His company is revolutionizing the dental field.

Speaker and motivator, he holds the world record of writing 100 books in 4 years accumulating many world records (to be officialized). Before that he held the world record of writing 9 books over 12 months, then, 15 books within 15 months to set the bar even higher with the world record of 36 books written within 18 months + 1 week.

By his second author anniversary, he scored his new landmark world record of 48 books within 24 months. And then 72 books in 36 months. By the 4th anniversary Dr. Bak scored his usually landmark of writing 96 books over 48 months, but he pushed even further, scoring also the new world record of 100 books written within 4 years!

His books are covering:

- **ENTREPRENEURSHIP**
- **LEADERSHIP**
- **QUEST OF IDENTITY**
- **DENTISTRY AND MEDICINE**
- **PARENTING**
- **CHILDREN BOOKS**
- **PHILOSOPHY**

In 2003, he founded Mdex, a dental company upon which in 2018, he launched the most ambitious private endeavour to reform the dental industry, Canada wide. Philosopher, he has close to his heart the quest of happiness of the people surrounding him, patients and colleagues alike. In 2020, he launched an International collaborative initiative named **THE ALPHAS** to share knowledge and for Entrepreneurs and Doctors to thrive through the Greatest Pandemic and Economic depression of our time.

In 2016, he co-found with Tranie Vo, Emotive World Incorporated, a tech research company to use technology to empower happiness and sharing. U.A.X. the ultimate audio experience is the landmark project on which the team is advancing, utilizing the technics of the movie industry and the advancement in ARTIFICIAL INTELLIGENCE to save the book industry and to upgrade the continuing education space.

These projects have allowed Dr. Nguyen to attract interests from the international and diplomatic community and he is now the centre of a global discussion in the wellbeing and the future of the health profession. It is in that matter that he shares his thoughts and encourages the health community to share their own stories.

> "It's not worth it go through it alone! Together, we stand, alone, we fall."

Motivational speaker and serial entrepreneur, philosopher and author, from his own words, Dr. Nguyen describes himself as a dentist by circumstances, an entrepreneur by nature and a communicator by passion.

He also holds recognitions from the Canadian Parliament and the Canadian Senate.

From Canada, **William Bak**, is an 12 years old prodigy. At the age of 8 years old, he co-wrote a series of chicken books with his dad, Dr. Bak. Together, they are changing the world, one mind at a time, writing books for kids. So far, they have 32 books together.

He co-wrote the 11 chicken books in ENGLISH and then, had to translate his own books in FRENCH. This is how he has 22 chicken books. William also co-wrote 2 parenting books with his dad, Dr. Bak, THE BOOK OF LEGENDS volumes 1, 2 and 3; the first volume of THE RISE OF LEGENDS; 2 Vaccine books (French and English); TIMING, William first Apollo Protocol book. Lately, William has also wrote his first book solo at the age of 11, PAPA, J'SUIS PAS CON and the PROLOGUES OF DESTINY, volume 1 and 2, and AU PAYS DES PAPAS 1 and 2.

To promote his books, William embraced the stage for the first time in 2019 talking to a crowd of 300+ people. Since, he has appeared in many videos to talk about his books and upcoming projects.

In the midst of COVID, he got bored and started his YOUTUBE CHANNEL : GAMEBAK, reviewing video games.
By the end of 2020, he has joined THE ALPHAS as the youngest anchor of the upcoming world project COVIDCONOMICS in which he will give his perspective and host the opinions of his generation.

"I will show you. I won't force you. But I won't wait for you."
- William Bak and Dr. Bak

Writing with his Dad, William holds world records to be officialized:

- The youngest author writing in 2 languages
- Co-author of 8 books within a month
- The first kid to have written 20 children books
- The child to have written his first solo book in 9 days
- The first child who wrote 33 books within 43 months

THE RISE OF LEGENDS
TO THE MOON AND BEYOND
by Dr. BAK NGUYEN & WILLIAM BAK

INTRODUCTION
BY Dr. BAK NGUYEN

THE REBOOT BEFORE THE NEW YEAR
CHAPTER 1- Dr. BAK NGUYEN
JUST WHEN I WAS ABOUT TO GIVE UP

THE VACCINE
CHAPTER 2- Dr. BAK NGUYEN & WILLIAM BAK
A TALE OF SPIES AND ALIENS

THE COMEBACK
CHAPTER 3- WILLIAM BAK
WE GOT OUR MAGIC BACK

LEGENDS OF DESTINY
CHAPTER 4- Dr. BAK NGUYEN
500 CHARACTERS

PROLOGUES OF DESTINY
CHAPTER 5- Dr. BAK NGUYEN & WILLIAM BAK
ETO, THE WINGLESS ANGEL

LEGENDARY
CHAPTER 6- WILLIAM BAK
IN 3 WORDS, I LOVE IT!

HISTORY REPEATS ITSELF
CHAPTER 7- Dr. BAK NGUYEN
THE STORM OF MOMENTUM

PAPA, I'M NOT AN IDIOT
CHAPTER 8- WILLIAM BAK
MY FIRST SOLO BOOK

I BEAT MY DAD AT HIS OWN GAME
CHAPTER 9- WILLIAM BAK
I AM SO PROUD!!!

TRIBUTES
CHAPTER 10- Dr. BAK NGUYEN
TO HONOUR YOUR PARENTS

PAPALAND
CHAPTER 11- Dr. BAK NGUYEN & WILLIAM BAK
THE CHRISTMAS TALES

WE ARE NOT GIVING UP
CHAPTER 12- WILLIAM BAK
BUT IT WAS PAINFUL

THE GAMES AND THE ELVES
CHAPTER 13- Dr. BAK NGUYEN
THE SHOW MUST GO ON

THE BOOK OF ELVES
CHAPTER 14- Dr. BAK NGUYEN & WILLIAM BAK
GAME ON

WE PLAYED THE STORY
CHAPTER 15- Dr. BAK NGUYEN
I LOVE VIDEO GAMES

WE DID IT AGAIN
CHAPTER 16- Dr. BAK NGUYEN
WE SURFED OUR MOMENTUM

AU PAYS DES PAPAS 2
CHAPTER 17- Dr. BAK NGUYEN & WILLIAM BAK
I CAN'T BELIEVE THAT WE MADE THIS ON HAPPENED

THIS IS NOT THE END
CHAPTER 18- WILLIAM BAK
AND WHAT IS NEXT?

CONCLUSION
BY Dr. BAK NGUYEN

Dr. BAK's ANNEX

INTRODUCTION

by Dr. BAK NGUYEN

It has been weeks since I last wrote something new. The last book I wrote was **AU PAYS DES PAPAS 2**. That introduction was written about 2 months ago. That said, I did not sit on my hand since. For the last month, I got 4 books published on Amazon, Kindle, and Apple Books, in COMBO version.

For those still wondering, COMBO is a format that I am currently the only author to have access to: to publish a paperback book with a code to access the audiobook version of the same book. So in other words, I also produced 4 audiobooks last month!

My world records titles are on the number of books I wrote, not the number of books published or audiobooks produced. Well, that's just sad since those are all now part of my production process.

On that note, with the Alpha Co-authors of **ALPHA DENTISTRY** submitting their corrections, I will finally publish book #109, **ALPHA DENTISTRY volume 1, DIGITAL ORTHODONTICS**, the Assembled version. That one took more than 6 months to complete. Sure it is the world's first crowdsourcing for both orthodontics and dentistry, and there will be a before and after that book… but still, it does not help with my numbers for setting new landmark world records.

Actually, I finished last year with 100 books written in 4 years. By the 1st day of July this year, so 2 months before the end of my writing year, I have 108 books to show. Even if I never slowed down, the change in writing style (embracing fiction and international collaborations) added to the production of COMBO books (paperback and audiobook) with some **UAX** albums have greatly slowed down the birth of new titles.

About **UAX** albums, which are blockbuster audiobooks productions, since the end of **THE BOOK OF LEGENDS volume 3,** we released 4 albums distributed by Apple Music, Spotify, Amazon Prime, and all the major digital outlets.

Just to make it crystal clear, **UAX** and COMBO formats are both exclusive to my brand and are world's firsts. I've pushed for the adoption of a new class of albums and content. Now, the UAX albums are available on streaming. Since the beginning, I have a total of 7 **UAX** albums. And again, those are not part of my world records…

To be honest, I haven't announced anything yet, but I am thinking of maybe not setting the next landmark world record of 120 books written in 5 years, and that would already be cheating since I got 4 extra from last year…

I am still hesitating. That's bad, really bad for someone fuelling on emotions and advancing through momentums. All of that to say how happy I am to be here with you, doing what I do best, writing new lines, new worlds, and paving the way for new adventures.

I woke up this morning with the notification that my first Parenting Trilogy, **THE BOOK OF LEGENDS** (volume 1, 2, and 3) co-written with William, is now available through the biggest International markets. Except for the first volume, which was published before I had my COMBO production in place, volume 2 and 3 are available in e-version, paperback and audiobook.

Actually, volume 2 was written in 2019, and volume 3 from 2019-2021. They were never published. I did that last month, revising the manuscripts, editing and publishing them both. I submitted volume 3 yesterday, by the end of the afternoon to Amazon. To have Apple and Amazon publish my books within hours of their submission was my first real empowerment.

"TO KEEP MOMENTUM, GO FOR YOUR NEXT WIN,
AS SOON AS POSSIBLE, NO MATTER HOW BIG OR SMALL THAT WIN IS."
DR. BAK NGUYEN

Well, that kept me on track to keep producing. Thank you Apple, thank you Amazon. Lately, my fan base is also more and more vocal about the inspiration that I am providing to them. I received more and more testimonies and thank you notes from, to me, almost complete strangers. They may be strangers to me, but to them, I have been part of their lives for months if not years by now.

For the last 5 years, my trusted lieutenant and brother, Jonas Diop has been pushing me to mentor people on a large scale. I always resisted the temptation for 2 reasons:

1. I had already too much to do on my plate
2. I do not know how good of a mentor I could be

Well, my plate is fuller than ever, post-pandemic, trying to keep my company afloat and with my head already underwater trying to keep up with the next world record to set. Lately, the massive recruitment of anchors and leaders in the International Dental community, joining the Alphas as co-authors gave me a boost in confidence about my leadership and my impact.

Then, the testimonies and thank you notes pushed me to embrace what I have become, without me noticing: a public face and someone people are looking up to. The last note I received was particularly moving. It was the thank you letter of a patient I empowered and supported throughout very difficult times as she was trying to regain her medical titles and her her stripes as a physician after having immigrated. Well, 2 days ago, she wrote back saying thank you and that she made it!!!!

So I may be short from my own expectations, but I am way above what I thought of myself. On that, I have all of you to thank. You empowered me to be much greater than who I am! On that note, I have finally said yes to mentoring people on a large scale, in Dr. Bak's style.

I will be doing so with the proximity that I like, talking as I look into your eyes and sharing a private space. Those sessions will be virtual and public within the community of Alphas. The first season will be composed of 24 sessions of 1 hour each over the course of a year. The first session is scheduled to start in less than 2 weeks.

So how about this year's announcement? Will I try to push to 120 books or will I simply give up setting the next landmark world record? To be fair, whatever my numbers will be, it will still be a world record, but maybe not a landmark.

With the mentoring sessions starting, a idea is growing slowly in the back of my head.

> "IF IT TOOK ME 4 YEARS TO WRITE 100 BOOKS,
> HOW LONG WILL IT TAKE ME TO LAUNCH 100 AUTHORS?"
> DR. BAK NGUYEN

That would be a hell of an announcement and a new landmark challenge. It is not official yet, but since I wrote that down in this book, I guess that it is coming soon, at least amongst the Alphas.

And amongst these authors, who is the first? Who is my first protege and biggest success? William Bak! The trilogy of the **BOOK OF LEGENDS** is telling that story, one about a father and a son finding each other. Within 4 years, William has become a multiple world records author with 32 books as co-author and 1 in solo. We finished the last book (volume 3) with much mysteries, not knowing what would come next.

Well, I am happy and proud to announce today the beginning of a new trilogy, after the trilogy of **THE BOOK OF LEGENDS**. This is the first volume of **THE RISE OF LEGENDS, to the moon and beyond**!

Welcome to the Alphas.

I will show you.
I won't force you.
But I won't wait for you.
Dr. Bak Nguyen
& William Bak

CHAPTER 1
"THE REBOOT BEFORE THE NEW YEAR"
by Dr. Bak Nguyen

It's been months, more than 12 since I tried to launch William on a new series of books: ANGELS AND DEMONS. I gave him the lead, I was very, very patient, and yet, nothing happened. Just to keep the air from drying off, we wrote the last instalment of the CHICKEN BOOKS: **CHICKEN FOREVER**.

That was hard and mostly unpleasant. For sure, the magic was gone. Sure, it was COVID and the morale was very, very low, not just at home, but across the board and across the universe. Is that an excuse?

I wish I could do something to overturn the general vibe, but the only thing I could do was to work on myself. Even during COVID, I did not stop pushing for more and more landmark world records. That year, I set the landmark world record of writing 72 books over 36 months. That was a huge win, especially since I was now in the sight of the financial and medical international elite.

They saw my posts, they read my goals, and before they had the time to doubt, they witnessed Amazon and Apple Books carrying out my new titles, one after the next. I was nominated and elected by peers into the World's Top100 doctor 2021.

So was COVID that bad? COVID was a huge liability to me. But since I know how to leverage my liabilities, it was not easy, but I managed to elevate myself from the challenges and the depression. Today, I am amongst the most influential dentists in the world!

That was me. What about William? Well, COVID got the best of my son. He was demotivated, struggled with addiction to online games, and turned dark from the bad influence of the people he connected with online. Of his genius and the cute prodigy, most were now eclipsed by bad habits and vain attitudes. I did my best to keep him motivated, but he was slipping, and slipping fast.

By Christmas 2020, we both concluded that ANGELS AND DEMONS won't happen. That would be the first time that we will be giving up.

We celebrated Christmas in confinement, not making more ripples. The fish was dead in the water and I had to accept that. 2021 was about to start and I just needed to flush 2020 down the toilets for good and hope for better, by the dawn of 2021.

We all know that 2021 would be even worse than 2020, but by that time, I, and most of the world, were hoping. I was looking forward to what would come next? What new book I will be writing next?

> "MAKE LEVERAGE OUT OF YOUR LIABILITIES
> TO KEEP MOVING FORWARD..."
> DR. BAK NGUYEN

To compensate for the lack of family reunions and celebrations, Tranie decided to spend as much time as possible enjoying the outdoor and embracing the Canadian winter.

It is during one of these one-day outdoor activities that William started to question me about what a vaccine was. Vaccine, that was a word that was circulating more and more.

By the end of 2020, there was no controversy yet about the **vax** and the **non-vax**, we were still one nation, only divided by our views on races, religions, and everything else in between. Vaccination was mostly a subject of interest, bearing the hope that life will be resuming to normal soon.

Because William asked the questions, I had to answer. Then, I listen to my own answers and it hit me: make leverage of each of your liabilities! I wrote down the questions and, during the ride driving home, I tested my answers with William, to see what a 10 year old could understand.

> "THIS IS SCIENCE, IN WORDS THAT YOU'LL UNDERSTAND."
> DR. BAK NGUYEN

It was pretty late when we finally got home, but the fire of inspiration was revived again, and I could not take the chance to let it fade away, even slightly. I started writing his questions and my answers.

I used words and metaphors to make sure that any child from 5 and above would understand what a vaccine is. Not the specific vaccine for COVID, but of any vaccine. Younger, I read the book for kids describing Louis Pasteur, the inventor of the first vaccine, with a giant syringe in his hand, introducing an army of soldiers to find the bacteria.

That was nearly 40 years ago. To that day, it is still what helped me understand the basis of the idea of a vaccine. As a result, I was never afraid of receiving a vaccine. Yeah, I am also a doctor, but Louis Pasteur and his soldiers helped a lot!

Then, I also realized that I was not the only one inspired by that war-like theme to describe how our bodies react. Throughout dental school, that is how every single professor was comparing the body to an army standing against the invaders.

So I embraced that trend and pushed the comparison to the extreme, making a reboot of the tale of Louis Pasteur, one without him in the tale.

COVID cost me my hopes and business expansions. It stalled and threatened my business and mental health. Unless I missed something, that is the definition of a liability. So I will leverage COVID to get back on track!

I got the short children's book out within 24 hours. I even asked my friend and mentor, Dr. Jean De Serres, formal president of Hema Quebec (our equivalent of the RED CROSS) to revise my answers and explanations. And **THE VACCINE**, our 77th title was born, just before the new year!

Since the subject was a hot topic and one of the utter most importance, I couldn't have only an English version available. William translated **THE VACCINE** within days in French. That became our 79th book, **LE VACCIN**, #78 was another book, **POWER PLAY**, a book I wrote on teamwork.

We received so much praise for our efforts to have simplified and explained what a vaccine is to kids. I was so encouraged by the general reception, that I got Brenda Garcia, one of my trusted lieutenants, to translate the whole book into Spanish. **LA VACUNA** was numbered 077B, since neither William nor myself had to work directly on it.

If **THE VACCINE** was signed in 2020, in early 2021, **LE VACCIN** and **LA VACUNA** were both available on the traditional networks, including Apple Books, Amazon, Kindle, and now, Barnes & Noble in COMBO version.

Our interests were such that I launched the production of **UAX** albums (Ultimate Audio Experience) to produce blockbuster audiobooks, today, streaming on Apple Music, Spotify, Amazon Prime, and all the other major digital outlets.

It made so much sense. Even if that was an insane amount of work, it went like a breeze. Because we had fun and because we were inspired. If I have to add another secret ingredient to the success, it was because we did not slow down, I built from every single win and grew it into momentum.

Well, **THE VACCINE** became our come back, as father and son, as the shock-duo writing books and History together. That endeavour really brought momentum and the magic back.

To this day, the 3 versions of **THE VACCINE**, its audiobooks, and their **UAX** albums are amongst our best sellers. I took my own medicine and leveraged myself out of failure and depression, leveraging my liabilities.

This is the first volume of **THE RISE OF LEGENDS, to the moon and beyond**!

Welcome to the Alphas.

> I will show you.
> I won't force you.
> But I won't wait for you.
> Dr. Bak Nguyen
> & William Bak

Dr. BAK NGUYEN WILLIAM BAK

THE VACCINE.
A TALE OF SPIES AND ALIENS

CHAPTER 2
"THE VACCINE"
by Dr. Bak Nguyen & William Bak

Here, I am proud to present to you, THE VACCINE, a tale of spies and aliens to demystify the word that every adult is currently throwing left and right, almost like headless chickens.

PROLOGUE
THE QUESTIONS

 his morning,
William, my 10-year-old son
Woke me up with a big question mark
on his forehead.

Papa, what is a vaccine?
And why should we have one?
Is it dangerous?
How does it work?

Is it the Coronavirus
That we are injecting ourselves with?
Can we die from it?

Papa, it doesn't make sense
To inject the Coronavirus in us, so why do it?

I don't know where that all came from,
But these were surely legitimate questions.

William, I know you have many questions.
Let's address them one by one,
Shall we?

"THERE ARE NO STUPID QUESTIONS, JUST STUPID ANSWERS."
- DR. BAK NGUYEN

If you could just let me
Brush my teeth first...

QUESTION #1
WHAT IS A VACCINE?

A vaccine is a solution
That medical professionals will inject
Into people to prevent them
From becoming sick.

It is an inactive piece of the virus
Called RNA that is injected into your body
So your body can form **antibodies**
To fight the real virus.

"HEIN???"
- WILLIAM BAK

You see William,
A virus is like an alien invasion,
When the aliens are coming in.
Our body needs their police forces
And army to stop them.

Most of the time,
The Aliens are obvious
And easy to recognize.

Some other times,
They are invisible to us
Or are in disguise,
Looking like the local population.

Then, like spies,
They infiltrate our bodies
And prepare their invasion.

So a vaccine is a way for our police forces

And army to identify and to target
The alien spies in disguise.

This is what a vaccine is,
From a science standpoint
Put into words you'll understand.

QUESTION #2
WHY DOES THE VIRUS WANT TO GET INTO OUR BODY?

The answer to this one is simple.
They are looking for a warm home.

Virus are much smaller than human
We are like a planet to them
They look at us and see a planet
One to explore
One to conquer

Our body is home to our cells
Cells are our population
Viruses are even smaller than cells,
Like any good alien invaders
They are getting inside of our cells
And taking over.

This is why, from the outside
Our cells cannot make the difference
Between a normal cell
And a contaminated one.

Once a cell gets contaminated
It becomes sick
And slowly will morph into a zombie
By then, they are easy to identify
But then, it might be too late.

This is why we need to deliver
The special package before the invasion
So our body has the time to train
And to create special units
Code named **ANTIBODIES**.

This is what a vaccine is,

From a science standpoint
Put into words you'll understand.

QUESTION #3
WHERE DO YOU GET THE VIRUS?

 ou can get the virus
From any entrances of your body
From your mouth, from your nose
From your eyes, from your ears
And even from your skin.

The virus is so small
That it can get in
From all of these places.

Your safe bet is to clean
Your hands often
And to wear a special mask
So you block the entrances.

Until you have a vaccine
And have a way to stop
The virus from getting inside of your body.

This is what a vaccine is,
From a science standpoint
Put into words you'll understand.

QUESTION #4
WHAT IS THE VIRUS DOING ONCE INSIDE OUR BODY?

nce inside of our body
The first virus will try
To establish a base.

They will infiltrate some of our cells
And regroup.
The viruses have no means of communication
So they cannot call for reinforcement

They are the invasion!
Now that they are in,
They stay discreet as spies
And identify what cells
To take over.

Then, once inside the cell
The virus will copy itself
To create his own squads of spies

If no one has arrested them yet
The spies will get out
And find new cells to infect
Each time, they find a cell,
They make a new base,
A new factory to make
More aliens like them.

If our police forces act on time
They surround the contaminated cells
Before they become zombies
And put them away.

If we act too late
Most of our cells will already be contaminated

And be either sick or zombies
By then, it might be too late
And the police forces will have to call the army

Once the army arrive
It is no joke.
They will torch all the cells of the neighbourhood
If that does not work,
They will be calling for a nuke

You do not want a nuke attack
Inside of your body.
This is only, if they get ran over by
The Zombies cells and the aliens inside.

This is what a vaccine is,
From a science standpoint
Put into words you'll understand.

QUESTION #5
WHY SHOULD WE GET VACCINATED?

 vaccine is a special package
For your body
To form **ANTIBODIES**
To fight the virus.

"HEIN???"
- WILLIAM BAK

It is a way for your army
To have special goggles
To see the alien spies
And to stop them.

Knowing who they are,
They won't be torching the entire neighbourhood,
But could now single out
Only the alien spies.

Would you refuse such tools
To your police forces?

If you refuse,
They will end up with nothing
To single out the alien spies
From the rest of your normal population of cells,

Either they will arrest
The wrong people, innocent people
Or they will fail at their task
Of protecting your body
And the alien spies will take over!

That's your choice!

This is what a vaccine is,
From a science standpoint
Put into words you'll understand.

QUESTION #6
IS IT DANGEROUS?

accines have been around for centuries
And have saved millions of people
From infections.

    You surely have received many vaccines
For the different viruses yourself.
You are strong and healthy, no?

In rare cases,
Some people develop adverse side effects
And there are complications.
But that is the exception,
Not the general rule.

Otherwise, we would all be dead by now
Since we have all been vaccinated.

> "SO, IS IT DANGEROUS???"
>   - WILLIAM BAK

When your soldiers
Receive the special equipment,
They must learn to use it
And to adapt their ways.

Since those are goggles
And special ammo,
Sometimes special bombs,
Some of your soldiers may get hurt
Learning how to use them.

Vaccines are weapons to fight aliens (virus),
They are not toys.
They are efficient.

Done respecting the safety protocol,
They are of good use
And will do much good.
Otherwise, they may cause harm.

In the case of the people
Getting sick from a vaccine,
It is not their fault,
We just need to find a way
So their body can understand
The safety protocol of the vaccine.

Not all bodies are talking the same tongue.

This is what a vaccine is,
From a science standpoint
Put into words you'll understand.

QUESTION #7
HOW DOES IT WORK?

ell, a vaccine is
An inactive part of a virus
Called RNA.

     Those will be injected
Into our bodies
And be copied to form
Detectors of that specific virus.
We call them, The **ANTIBODIES**.

> "SO THEY ARE THE ENEMIES OF OUR BODIES?"
> - WILLIAM BAK

No, there are the detectors
Identifying the enemies
And the alien spies.

The Antibodies are special units
Patrolling our body to arrest the virus.
If they identify one,
They attach themselves to it
And call for reinforcements.

Then, the police force will arrest
The alien spy (virus)
And put it away.

The special units
Are called **ANTIBODIES**.
The police forces and the army
Are called **WHITE CELLS**.

If the police arrests the alien spies,

They stop the invasion
And the war never happens.
This is when you do not get sick.
Otherwise, you might need bedtime
And hot noodle chicken soup.

This is what a vaccine is,
From a science standpoint
Put into words you'll understand.

QUESTION #8
IS IT WITH THE VIRUS THAT WE ARE INJECTING OURSELVES WITH?

s I said earlier,
We are injecting
Only a little piece of the virus,
Not the virus itself.

It's like having now
A heat signature of the alien spies
And a photography of their faces,

It does not mean
That we have opened the door
Or have granted them access
With a passport of any kind.

Only now, we know how they look like.
And our special forces might identify them
So our police forces
Can arrest them, the alien spies.

This is what a vaccine is,
From a science standpoint
Put into words you'll understand.

QUESTION #9
CAN WE DIE FROM THAT?

The answer is
There are risks of complications.

Some bodies won't be able to read
The safety protocol
And might react to the vaccine
As if it was the alien spy itself.

In that case,
Instead of creating a special unit
That will duplicate the photos
And the heat signature,
They will call in the army
And nuke the vaccine instead.

In a nuke, called **inflammation**
There is no distinction between
The aliens or the normal cell population
Everyone gets hurt.

The harm is the nuke
That they launched themselves
On the vaccine.

Rest assured,
There is no risk o,
But that does not
Happen often.

But it still happens sometimes.
This is why it is so important
That the safety protocols
Are delivered
And understood by

All our bodies

A vaccine is not the enemy
It is a way to create
Special units that will
Identify the alien spies
So our body won't nuke
Itself by mistake

"WHEN IS IT TOO LATE FOR A VACCINE?"
- WILLIAM BAK

A vaccine will only work
Before the virus get inside of your body
Or when very few spies are present

But once the zombie cells have appeared
It is too late for the vaccine
By then, you will have to call the army
And to nuke a few neighbourhoods of cells.

It is then that you will feel sick
That you will have a fever
And hopefully, after a few days
You will get better.

Your army will have wiped out the invasion

This is what a vaccine is,
From a science standpoint
Put into words you'll understand.

QUESTION #10
IT DOES NOT MAKE SENSE TO INJECT OURSELVES WITH THE VIRUS. SO WHY DO IT?

ell, you are right.
It does not make sense to inject
Ourselves with the Coronavirus.
A vaccine is not that.

Once more,
We are sending a special package
To our body so it can prepare itself
For the invasion

From the special package
They have the instruction and weapon
To train special units that will
Identify the alien spies specifically.

We are not sending alien spies
Into our body,
Just ways to identify them
And to prepare our troops,
The special units (**antibodies**)

This is what a vaccine is,
From a science standpoint
Put into words you'll understand.

QUESTION #11
CAN I EAT THE VACCINE INSTEAD OF HAVING AN INJECTION?

nfortunately, the vaccine
Need to be injected
Inside of your body
To be efficient.

If you put it in your mouth,
By eating it
Or drinking it
It won't work.

> "WHY PAPA, IT IS STILL GOING INSIDE YOUR BODY..."
> — WILLIAM BAK

Think of it this way,
You need to deliver
The special package
To the special unit's headquarters
Instead, if you eat it,
You are delivering it to the kitchen
How do you think that it will work?

After the kitchen, the toilet is next.
If you eat or drink the vaccine
Your special troops keep waiting
And never receive your envoy

> "REALLY PAPA, THE KITCHEN?"
> — WILLIAM BAK

Actually, it is your stomach

And the toilet is your intestine
It was just easier
To picture them that way.

In reality, once in your stomach
The vaccine will be digested
And decomposed like food
And the package will be terminated.
In that case, the aliens
Will be victorious.

Would you want that?
So do not eat nor drink
The vaccine!

This is what a vaccine is,
From a science standpoint
Put into words you'll understand.

QUESTION #12
IS THAT ALL TRUE PAPA? OR YOU ARE JUST PLAYING GAMES WITH ME?

This is all the truth.
I learned that becoming a doctor.
Even a dentist has to know
How a vaccine works.

I just put the explanations into
Words that you would understand easily,
Talking about special units,
Aliens spies, and invasion.

Actually, I am not that far from reality.
In med school,
We talked about virus infections
As invasions and we often compared
Our body and its defence reactions
As war measures.

Ask all doctors,
They will tell you their version of this story,
And the theme of war will always surface.
Why? Because it is what really happens
Inside our body,
A fight and a war to keep
The virus at bay.

And with this,
Most of his question marks were gone.
Now a new one appears on his face.

"PAPA, ARE YOU HUNGRY?"
- WILLIAM BAK

This is what a vaccine is,
From a science standpoint
Put into words you'll understand.

I will show you.
I won't force you.
But I won't wait for you.
Dr. Bak Nguyen
& William Bak

CHAPTER 3
"THE COMEBACK"
by William Bak

The vaccine was the key to remaking books. Lately, we lost a lot of motivation to write. The momentum was long gone. That's the truth. Part of it is my fault since I became addicted to online gaming. Between COVID and my addiction, it was very hard to get back to writing with my dad.

One morning, after we had fun outside the previous day, my dad asked me to his office. Sure, it is home, but my dad still has a very impressive, almost intimidating office. I got called there. I was a little confused, did I do something wrong? I wasn't sure.

It is then that he shared that he wanted to write a new book and he wanted me as a partner. He thought that this could reinforce our connection and get our magic back. We were both very aware of the challenge ahead since it would be hard to motivate me.

I love my dad and I miss the magical connection that we shared. So, of course, I said YES without hesitation. The only problem was that I had no clue what book to write! I thought that we were done with the chickens!

To keep my motivation, he proposed a deal that I could not refuse. For this book, I won't have to write, just to ask questions. That was a fantastic deal to keep me motivated. You see, talking is easy for me, I can talk for hours. Writing…, I know that I am good at, but I prefer talking by far.

Yesterday, we were in the car when I started asking questions about life. Amongst these questions, a few were about COVID. Well, these are the questions picking the interest of my dad. We went back on my questions and I got to ask new ones too. Each question would be a chapter. My job was to ask the questions about COVID, listen to the answers, and comment. That I can do, no problem!

My dad is fast, very fast when it comes to writing books. We managed to complete the book within 2 days or even less. It was not a new record for my dad (who has written a book in less than 24 hours) but for me, it was a first!

We celebrated the New Year with a big smile on our faces and with great hopes in our hearts. We were back in the game, the both of us, as co-authors. After that book, of course, I had to work on the translation in French while my dad had a surprise for me. He launched the production of **UAX** albums on these books, which are blockbuster movies without images.

I had so much fun listening to the tracks and how my dad made the story come to life! That kept me very motivated and I finished the French book within days too. Then, we asked a friend of my dad, Brenda to translate the book into Spanish. That was so awesome! It would be the first time that one of my books will be in Spanish! I really had a great time working on **THE VACCINE**.

After **THE VACCINE**, our momentum kept us surfing and **LEGENDS OF DESTINY** was next in line. That book is about Earth and another planet named Destiny. It is about elves, demons, angels, kings, and queens. We made more than 500 characters to populate that universe.

That is very much what it is, a whole universe! That's how much working on **THE VACCINE** has empowered our imagination and motivation.

"THE VACCINE WAS THE KEY TO FIXING OUR RELATIONSHIP AND WE DID IT IN 2 DAYS!"
WILLIAM BAK

My dad was so happy to have me back, writing books by his side. I did it and it was fun and easy. That's my kind of stuff, easy and fun stuff!

With **THE VACCINE**, we were back in the game. At least, I was. I know that my father never took his eyes off from the world records and kept scoring new landmarks. I am so happy to have written that book.

I really think that **THE VACCINE** will help kids around the world to understand what a vaccine really is and answer most of their questions as it did for me. I honestly think that it was the best educational book that we ever made.

More than the book, the **UAX** albums brought the experience to a whole other level. I loved the results but I loved, even more, the process. My dad got me involved to choose the music and the soundtracks. I decided if a sound would be added or not.

If you think that that is boring, think again. With sounds, we can make something normal, funny! I had so much fun doing the **UAX** albums with my dad as we were trying to include as many jokes as possible in the final mix.

I am not saying this because I worked on the **UAX** albums, but I really think that the **UAX** is the best medium to reach the kids and to educate them about something that, otherwise could be so dry and boring.

If you ask me, **THE VACCINE** was, so far, our best success! **UAX** elevated something great to an even greater status. In 4 letters, I would say: C.O.O.L, cool!

This is the second volume of the **BOOK OF LEGENDS**, the adventures continue... Welcome to the Alphas.

**I will show you.
I won't force you.
But I won't wait for you.**
Dr. Bak Nguyen
& William Bak

CHAPTER 4
"LEGENDS OF DESTINY"
by Dr. Bak Nguyen

It took about a month and a half to complete the production and the distribution of the 3 versions of **THE VACCINE**. The Spanish version was on its way and the **UAX** production started around the same time.

If the writing of **THE VACCINE** took literally 2 days, its French version took about a week, and the rest took much longer. We went from days to weeks. Still, that was the first time that I streamlined the whole process of writing to publishing to audiobook production to **UAX** albums, including their distributions.

By the end of February, all 3 versions were available internationally on all major platforms: books, streaming, downloadable, and paperback!

Were we back in business? It was surely very fun and easy, and as my friend Jonas would say, we were back in Momentum once more! I was happy, William was proud, and we weren't even tired!

I don't know about you, but every year, the end of January and the entire month of February are very hard on me. The lack of sun light, the Canadian cold weather, and by then, a year within COVID were taking their toll on my soul.

> "I WAS IMMUNE TO THAT SEASONAL DEPRESSION WITH THE VACCINE KEEPING ME IN MOMENTUM."
> DR. BAK NGUYEN

Since the beginning of COVID, I learnt to cook and spent much time watching streaming chefs. My favourite one is Gordon Ramsay and his show, HELL's Kitchen. I watched it with William because it was entertaining and, day after day, we picked up on the art of cooking.

To tell you the truth, that was not the best show to learn to cook, but because it was entertaining, it worked with us. So I started experimenting and cooking more and more plates. Especially when Tranie was recuperating from her back surgery, I was left in charge of the kitchen.

If my first plates were simple soups and 2 ingredients rice plates, within 12 months, pasta, lobsters, truffle oil, and Alfredo sauce were part of my lexicon. Surprisingly, my parents and in-laws loved my food!

There was not much to do during COVID to get out of the house once we were not working. Shopping at the grocery, cooking, and delivering food and plates to my parents and in-laws were my getaways. That and some nights riding with Tranie, just to remember how it felt to travel. But even that was restricted in curfew times.

So I was feeling better thanks to **THE VACCINE** and I was taking on my shoulders to share that positive energy. It was also during these months that the COVID vaccination campaign started. People were lining up for their dose. In the beginning, there was excitement and joy, the vaccine was the hope to resume life.

We were right on time and on pitch with the release of **THE VACCINE**. William and I were celebrating, watching more of Gordon Ramsay, discovering new alleys at the grocery store, and utilizing all of the new takeaway plates imposed by the government to all the restaurants.

Only one thing could simulate the feeling of joy and of satisfaction that I experience at the completion of each book. Believe it or not, it is when I cook, especially when it is time to plate the food in the reusable food containers that I saved from my takeaways. It is a beautiful experience each time. Then, I get to drive to my parents and in-laws to deliver my joy and new accomplishments.

> "COOKING, PLATING AND DELIVERING EXQUISITE MEALS TO THOSE I LOVE WERE THE NEW JOYS THAT I DISCOVERED WITHIN COVID."
> DR. BAK NGUYEN

It was during one of these deliveries, a Sunday evening, as I was driving with William when our next franchise came to us. We were only the 2 of us in the car, Tranie was busy with her task as COO of the company.

We talked about 2 different worlds, about Gods and about Kings. We laughed a lot and the essence of **LEGEND OF DESTINY** was born. That ride was magical, from the smell of the truffle oils to the sparkles in our minds.

We were still riding on our victory of **THE VACCINE** and I did not want to take the risk of falling back into the void we were stuck in for the last 2 years, with ANGELS AND DEMONS. I was more cautious this time.

The first thing that I learnt from the failure of ANGELS AND DEMONS was to not leave William in charge. I had to take charge, after all, I am the Momentum in our relationship. The second thing that I learnt was that my power comes from speed.

> **"I HAVE THE POWER OF SPEED THAT CAN RAISE MOMENTUM FROM THIN AIR TO DO THE IMPOSSIBLE, WITH EASE AND STYLE."**
> DR. BAK NGUYEN

In other words, *procrastination* will kill **LEGENDS OF DESTINY** just like it killed ANGELS AND DEMONS. As soon as I came back home, I started building. Not writing, building. I researched the internet and cast the heroes and characters of these 2 worlds, the same way I did with the chickens, buying royalty-free images.

I designed the logo and made collectible trading cards-like for each character. I got that idea from the hockey and baseball collectible cards that I bought when I was younger. Since all of it was digital, I pushed and I pushed with ease and fun. A week later, I had more than 500 characters and cards.

500 characters! I was overwhelmed myself. But the process was so fun and smooth. And the final result was breathtaking. I had 500 characters and their names. To not repeat the same mistakes of ANGELS AND DEMONS, I resisted the temptation to define their backstories right away.

I did that with William, or to William, to be more specific. That became our first book in this new franchise, **THE PROLOGUES OF DESTINY**, one describing the backstories, the universes, and grounding the principal elements to establish the future stories.

Actually, the writing of that book will only happen much later that year, after the completion of William's first solo book, **PAPA J'SUIS PAS CON** and my landmark world record of **100 books written in 4 years**.

Until then, I was still looking for ways to make this fun and to keep surfing the vibe of creativity. I spent much time researching ways to animate pictures and to add depth and life into 2D photos. I wrote a trailer introduction, selected a great soundtrack, and edited 2 groundbreaking trailers to keep our imagination sparkling.

That took about 2 months to research and to realize. Now, we had more than 500 characters, 2 cinematic trailers, soundtracks, and the time of our lives having fun.

It was the first time that we were adventuring in the realm of pure fiction with no educational nor philosophical purpose. If you need to know, those were the spines of each of my books. To draft on a new spine was a risky move and one that could break my momentum and inspiration.

Last time, with ANGELS AND DEMONS, I wanted to leverage William's fun to keep him motivated. Using his toys, he had fun for a few days and that was it. This time, I needed something stronger, much stronger.

First, for him to be involved, we divided the characters into 2 teams, his and mine. We picked one by one the characters in a draft-like to pick up our team, just like in gym class. I picked some of the characters he loved and he picked some of mine.

Then, we needed to define what these teams would be for. It is then that I decided to play their fate into video games, just like the Pokemon trading cards phenomenon.

In other words, we are not deciding who will survive our adventures, that will be decided in a round playing a video game. Do you have any idea how original and risky that is? We can end up losing our main hero and we will be then, stuck to fix the storyline! Just like they say in Hollywood, the show must go on!

So, to that point, we had 500+ breathtaking collectible cards divided into 2 teams. We resisted the temptation to define the characters more than with a name and description. Already, I could see William cracking with his envy to tell the backstories. By then, the backstories were so easy to write since we could use any one of the other characters to populate these storylines.

It was very organic, it was like the characters were taking a life of their own, interacting with one another. We were building a huge momentum and the **tension of creativity** was rising up. Then, I decided to push things to the next level, introducing William to an old classic strategy game that I was playing younger, STARCRAFT.

I had a DVD of the game at home but my computer had no more DVD drive. I went online and by chance, I found the game updated and live! It is still a huge phenomenon, even 20 years later.

We installed STARCRAFT 2 on 2 laptops and William, now 11, was having the time of his life. If for William it was magical and fun to discover leadership from the command centre, to me, it was a dive into **nostalgia**, a dive into an era where everything was possible and within reach, an era where I was writing fiction and never published, an era in which Hollywood was not a dream but a choice on the table.

There, you have them all, all of the secret ingredients we collected and used for the **LEGENDS OF DESTINY**. And I did not cook them right away. I prepped them and let them rest for 5 months on the back burner.

This is the first volume of **THE RISE OF LEGENDS, to the moon and beyond**!

Welcome to the Alphas.

I will show you.
I won't force you.
But I won't wait for you.
Dr. Bak Nguyen
& William Bak

LEGENDS OF DESTINY

Dr. Bak Nguyen   William Bak

Prologues of Destiny
volume one

CHAPTER 5
"PROLOGUES OF DESTINY"
by Dr. Bak Nguyen

After the failure to launch ANGELS AND DEMONS last year, this is our comeback. We changed the details of the story of the angel Eto but we kept the name and the character.

Following is the origin story of Eto, chapter 6 of the 1st volume of **LEGENDS OF DESTINY: PROLOGUES OF DESTINY**.

Eto, the wingless Angel
by William Bak

As the war ravaged the whole of creation, Ethem, the primal life force, created from its breath, the Angels, the guardians of balance. Angels are shapeless and can embody the shape of their choosing, changing shape at will.

The only limitation is that Angels can only take one shape from each species. Each time that they took a shape, they can morph but if they return into the shape of that species, they will reassume their previous form, along with the wounds and the scars.

In that sense, even if Angels are as powerful as some Gods, they are not invulnerable. Once an Angel is wounded, he or she can change into another shape to recuperate but will have burned down one shape to change into, unless the angel is willing to span the time and energy to heal that particular shape.

In other words, angels have as many lives as there are species in the creation. Since they are guardians and fighters, being wounded in battle is a hazard coming with their nature. This is also why Angels can be found in all shapes of life.

Since Ethem created the Angel from its breath, each Angel is unique. Each of them has a power to discover. Adrian's power is to absorb the energy around him, making him the most powerful Angel of all.

Not all Angels know their power. They are strong, simple-minded, but most still have to discover their power as they are keeping the balance of the Universe.

That day, there was a competition amongst the Angels to know who was the fastest. Lucifer, Erikiel, and Ethel were amongst the contestants. It was a friendly race, nonetheless, a brutal one. They ran and fought to find out who was the champion of the day.

Lucifer won the race but he still wanted to race more. Looking around, he pointed out Eto, the youngest of the Angels. "Why won't you race with me?" Eto hesitated for a long moment, he was easily impressionable.

He also knew that the real contest was not about speed but about strength. Everyone knew that the strongest was Adrian, so, to not upset their Lord, they found other themes in which to compete. Nothing good will come out of that, Eto was convinced.

Eto is young, small, and hasn't found his unique power yet. He is often looked at by the other Angels as weak. He does not like them much, but Ethel, the beautiful and kind Ethel. Ethel knew the power she had over Eto.

Ethel approached and whispered into Eto's ears: "Beat Lucifer and I will kiss you…" That was more than enough to motivate the shy Angel.

The Angels raced again. Lucifer, Erikiel, Eto, and even the beautiful Ethel. Every single Angel beat Eto twice at racing, even Ethel. It is then that Hermes, the Angel Executor, amongst the strongest of Angels after Adrian, told Eto what he really raced for. Since he is useless and weak, he will be serving as a messenger.

Amongst the tasks of Angels, warriors and guardians were the most envious positions to hold after those in command as Lord and Executor. Messenger was the last thing that any Angel likes to do.

Eto has been tricked by Ethel. She knew that Lucifer and Erikiel will beat her, that's why she pushed him into the contest too. Just as she approached to kiss him, even if he lost, Hermes told her that she too, will serve as a messenger since they seem to get along.

Ethel went mad! She wasn't happy about it but, in front of Hermes, she bowed down. Since that day, she despises Eto, the weak Angel. Despite that hate, Ethel kept Eto close to her to do most of the messaging work in her place. Eto, blinded by her beauty, did them all.

The war lasted for so long. Even with the creation of the Angels, the balance was not reestablished in the Universe. First Adrian ordered the Angels to destroy all the temples and to seize the portals. That weakened much the Gods who lost their means, sacrifices, and gold.

But that wasn't enough to keep balance. Tired of fighting for ions, Adrian came to the conclusion that for the war to end, one side must be eliminated, completely.

Adrian was the most powerful of the Angels, the Lord Angel and supreme commander. But to that order, his second in command, Erikiel, the Guardian, asked if that was not contrary to their mission to keep balance.

Adrian turned around, even without removing his helmet, and concentrated his attention on Erikiel who went dry within an instance. Erikiel was Adrian's most trusted lieutenant. That did not help him. Adrian kept coming closer and closer until Erikiel screamed his pain with only the echo of his voice.

Adrian drained all of the *grace* of Erikiel, leaving a dark cold corpse behind. No Angels dared to challenge the Angel Lord ever again. They did not dare to challenge the Lord Angel but many did not agree with him. Not about the murder of Erikiel but about their loyalty to Ethem and their true mission, to safeguard the balance of the Universe. How can the extermination of one side rimes with balance?

So the Angels started to defect and not just the less important Angels, but Archangels too like Lucifer and Ezechiel. They went into hiding. Adrian was furious and sent his armies to seek and punish the traitors.

Adrian dispersed Eto to look for Lucifer. Eto travelled the 4 corners of the Universe looking for the Archangel. He found him in the shape of a dragon. Eto knew that it was Lucifer. He never really like the Archangel but he did not agree with Adrian's decision either. He passed by the dragon, faking not to recognize his old pal.

Back in Heaven, he had to report to Hermes about his failure to locate Lucifer. In the courtyard was Ethel, also back from her mission to locate Ezechiel, which she did. Ezechiel was in chains and waiting to be presented to Adrian for punishment.

Hermes did not think much of Eto. He was in a hurry to present Ezechiel to his Lord Adrian. He told both Ethel and Eto to follow him to the courtroom. Adrian did not blink twice, sucking out the life of Ezechiel as he did to Erikiel.

When he asked what about Lucifer, Eto advanced, shaking and clapping his teeth. He bowed down and said that he did not find Lucifer. Adrian was mad and was about to drain the life out of Eto too, when Hermes intervened.

"My Lord, I am running very thin on Angels. Can we spare this one? There are still so many fugitives to look for." And as soon as he said these words, bow his head down not to provoke the wrath of Adrian.

It is then that Adrian remembered the unique power of Ethel, to know the truth from a single look. He asked Ethel if Eto was worth saving? Within an instant, she saw through Eto and his lies. She never loved Eto but she also came to get attached to him. She told the Angel Lord that Eto was useless but loyal… even if she knew that Eto was lying about Lucifer.

They were both sent out of the courtroom. Eto approached Ethel to thank her to have saved his life. Ethel, the kind and beautiful Angel changed face and tone completely and told Eto that from now on, she owns him. She knows that he found Lucifer disguised as a dragon and did not report that back.

Eto was crushed. He always thought that Ethel loved him and because of that, she protected him. He couldn't hold it anymore. They started screaming at each other. As they were arguing, Adrian heard everything.

He went out and served a warning to all the Angels: He and he alone owns the service of the Angels. He threw a lighting ball on Ethel who immediately started to burn.

Seeing Ethel screaming in pain, Eto raised his sword and went for the head of Adrian. Adrian from the back of his hand knocked down in a single blow the rebellious Eto. That gave just enough time for Ethel to flee while screaming.

Adrian was mad. So many traitors amongst the Angels. He decided that Eto will serve his role as messenger, one that all Angels will remember for eternity. He got Eto imprisoned and trialed.

No one dares to defend Eto, so his judgment was very quick. Adrian spared the life of Eto but for his crimes, Eto will have his wings amputated. To an Angel, there was no worse punishment, even worse than death. Without their wings, Angels cannot fly nor change shape anymore.

They can still live forever until they are killed. But living forever without wings is worse than death. Eto got his wings cut in front of all the remaining Angels.

This is **Prologues of Destiny, volume one**, the first trilogy.

I will show you.
I won't force you.
But I won't wait for you.
Dr. Bak Nguyen
& William Bak

CHAPTER 6
"LEGENDARY"
by William Bak

Well, the first time that we started thinking about angels and demons was 3 years ago. But we let that go for 2 years without any tangible progress. Finally, it came back on the table from a conversation in the car.

That was last year, as within the time of a car ride delivering food to my grandparents, me and my father started playing around with the idea of starting a new franchise. That's how **LEGENDS OF DESTINY** was born.

We just finished the books and all of the albums of **THE VACCINE** in all 3 languages, English, French, and Spanish. I remembered the first time I heard it streaming from the iPhone, straight from Spotify, it was magical.

We were back in the game, and about something else than chicken books! The funny thing is that **LEGENDS OF DESTINY** happened as we were **Uber eating** food that my father cooked to all 4 of my grandparents. That was the last thing that I expected from that ride.

To be honest, I was a little tired and bored of the educational books. I know that those are important and all, but I did my share. Now, I wanted to have fun, pure fun! Well, that's how my dad came up with the idea of writing a story between 2 different planets, with elves, humans, gods, and, of course, angels and demons.

That was not the recycling of our failed project, but a fresh new one. The only thing we kept from our failure was the angel Eto, which we borrowed from an old script of my father, one that he never published and wrote some 20 years ago.

I wanted fun, fantasy, with real heroes holding shields and swords. We did try that with **ANGELS AND DEMONS** and it did not work. So I told my dad that I wanted to break all the rules. I wanted them to fight with swords but also to have spaceships, guns, and advanced tech.

My dad said that it would not make sense, unless we set the actions on 2 different planets, and travelling between them, our heroes could also arrive in different timelines. To travel between time and planets, that was a really cool concept. I got hooked right away!

The planet DESTINY was just created, at least in our minds. Destiny is 10 times bigger than Earth, it is far, far away, in another galaxy, and its inhabitants are elves and orcs. I was so happy that finally, we would have fun making up new stories.

We talked about the heroes, the series of books, the different worlds and so much more. My dad was traumatized by what happened with **ANGELS AND DEMONS**, so he was very careful to not make the same mistakes. He took a whole week to draft the different characters, main and accessory. Everyone, he treated with the same attention. Actually, while he was drafting the characters, we did not know who were the heroes and who were the bad guys. Anything was possible!

A week later, he was so into it that he created more than 500 characters! We made them into a card-playing game and divided the characters into 2 teams, mine and his. We picked the character one by one, just like picking up the players of a sport team at school.

I had much fun playing that game. My dad's hope was that I got more and more attached to my characters and would fight for them! And fought I have. This is where it really became a game.

We had our team and every time that we wrote about a characters at the crossroad of life and death, we have to play for his or her survival. In other words, I had to fight my dad by playing video games to defend my characters. If I lost, my character could die. So it was also for the fate of my dad's characters.

With these rules, we do not write the whole story. We set up the world, got our characters to interact, and then, had to live with the consequences of the **DUELS**. More than one, I lost one of my heroes. My dad laughed for the first minutes but very quickly, turned around to face the consequences of that loss with me: how can we keep the story going if we just lost our main hero?

And that's what kept the writing of **LEGENDS OF DESTINY** so interesting. And you wonder which games we played? Well, MOBILE LEGENDS on the iPhone was one of our favourites. Later on, my dad introduced an old classic, STARCRAFT 2. I must tell you that since the beginning of this franchise, I had so much fun, playing, writing, and fixing the storylines.

We decided that there would be, not one, but 3 trilogies to this series. I am not sure how that happened. That surely sounded like much, much work, but I did not care since all I wanted was to start the first book, right away!

It took my dad a few months to work on elaborating the universes, making 2 movie-like trailers (I don't know how he pulled that one out, but he managed to edit 2 Hollywood trailers to motivate us). To be honest, I was already pumped up. I think that the trailers were more for him.

Only after he set his landmark world record of 100 books written within 4 years and me, after I finished my first solo book, that we wrote and released within days the first volume of the series: **PROLOGUES OF DESTINY**.

Writing that book was so fun and easy since it was about describing the backstories of the main characters, establishing the different worlds, and how they interact with one another.

I especially love the chapter about Kal, the old God of fire. That one tied together the logic and the bridges between Earth and Destiny. At that stage, I was living the legends! We also made the **UAX** album of **PROLOGUES OF DESTINY** right away, just like we did with **THE VACCINE**.

> "IF A BOOK MAKES IT REAL, A UAX ALBUM BRINGS EVERYTHING TO LIFE."
> WILLIAM BAK

It was more than a dream come true to me. It was bigger than in my wildest dream. We were writing our version of **LORD OF THE RINGS** and **GAMES OF THRONES** combined! It is that epic, trust me! This could be our next big hit! Like Harry Potter, it all started with a book, no?

Well, who knows what **LEGENDS OF DESTINY** will become. A series of blockbusters? A hit television show? Let's start with a best-selling series of books, shall we? In 3 words: I love it!

This is the first volume of **THE RISE OF LEGENDS, to the moon and beyond**!

Welcome to the Alphas.

I will show you.
I won't force you.
But I won't wait for you.
Dr. Bak Nguyen
& William Bak

CHAPTER 7
"HISTORY REPEATS ITSELF"
by Dr. Bak Nguyen

That was around the end of my 4th year of writing as an author. The previous year, I set the landmark world record of writing 72 books within 36 months. This year, I was looking at 96 books to keep my momentum.

Well, my Alpha friend, Dr. Paul Ouellette launched the idea that I should reach 100 to make a bold statement. It was a joke and friendly empowerment, but he was absolutely right! That would be bold!

And so, I set my mind to reach 100 books before the end of that summer (August). Just for fun! By July, I was still travelling Canada for the series **COVIDCONOMICS**. I was 9 books short of 100. To set that year's landmark record would seem mission impossible.

Fortunately, I paced myself to the Olympic Summer games in Tokyo. I was following the swimmers and to each of their stroke, I had a word down. It was tight but I reached the finished line right on time: 100 books written within 4 years, topping my own world record pace!

Needless to say how exhausted I was after that challenge. Well, to celebrate, William asked me:

- Papa, how long it took you to write your first book?
- 14 days. Why do you ask?
- Well, if I write 1 chapter per day, I will finish in 8 days and I will have beaten you, right?
- Not quite William. You still have an introduction and a conclusion to add.
- So, if I write a chapter of 500 words a day, in 10 days, I would have beaten you?
- What?! Are you looking to write your first solo book?
- I am not sure, but I am thinking of it!
- That would be the best gift ever to celebrate my new landmark of 100 books over 4 years. What will you be writing about?

We both remembered that 5 years earlier, William wanted to write 2 books. One about the lion heart and one about being a good son. Well, the lion heart became the 22 chicken books. The book about being a good son, that one, we never wrote. How about writing that book?

The title of how to be a good son was lacking appeal. We spent an evening playing with the idea and I proposed: **PAPA, J'SUIS PAS CON**, the French title meaning **PAPA, I'M NOT AN IDIOT**. We laughed the rest of that evening.

I even wrote the lyrics of a song for the occasion. Here's the translation:

PAPA, I'M NOT AN IDIOT

Stupid, stupid, stupid
Papa, I'm not an Idiot
I know that sometimes, I can be dumb
It's not my fault
It happens that I don't have all of my head

No, papa, nothing is wrong
Why are you always so serious?
Are you really happy?
You are always telling me about my attitude
And each day, you criticize my habits

I know how much you love me
But it is always me saying, I love you
Each day, you tell me to eat lettuce
You say to be open, but I am lost
Papa, I try very hard
But I need some space

Papa, I'm not an Idiot
Papa, I'm not stupid, no I'm not stupid,
Oops, I'm stupid. Ok, just this once.

Papa, why aren't you happy?
You know that I can't always be smart
And for you, I ate a ball in my face
I am trying my best, but some days, it is very hard

Papa, I'm not an Idiot
Papa, I'm not stupid, no I'm not stupid,
Oops, I'm stupid. Ok, just this once.

I have to go to bed
But I am not tired yet
And I have to eat all of my carrots
I'm the child, so it is always my fault

Papa, you are my best friend,
But some days, you make it very hard
You know how much I hate radishes
And for you, I ate them too.
Now I look like an imbecile

Papa, I'm not an Idiot
Papa, I'm not stupid, no I'm not stupid,
Oops, I'm stupid. Ok, just this once.

That was my gift to him, to start him on his new challenge and momentum. William will write that story, his first solo book within 9 days, beating me as I took 14 days to write my first book.

Sure, I have to correct and rewrite most of his words for the final version, but he did it, in 9 days! I was so proud of my son. I could not have wished for a better gift to celebrate my new landmark world record.

It was only then that I realized that History was repeating itself: as I set my first landmark world record of writing 15 books in 15 months, William asked me about the book that I promised to write with him. That was 3 years ago.

We now know what happened next, we set landmark world records upon landmark world records, as father and son. I was not the one pushing him, he was the one pushing me! Now, as I set my new landmark world record, he raised the bar, beating me at my own game.

By September 9, his chapters were all in. I spent the next week correcting and rewriting his chapters. Sometimes, 500 words became 2000 words, but the essence was all his. I just embellished and gave more details to his writing.

Before the end of September, we were holding his book in our hands. Even Audible accepted the publication of that book at a much faster pace than I was used to. That was right after I was out of breath crossing the finished line of 100 books!

> "WILLIAM RECHARGED ALL OF MY BATTERIES AND SET THE COURSE FOR THE MOON AND BEYOND."
> DR. BAK NGUYEN

The last time he did that, I broke the sound barrier, going from 15 books over 15 months to 36 books in 18 months + 1 week. What will this time bring?

I don't have the answer to that question. By then, I also knew better than to set expectations and to kill the vibe. I just enjoyed and let it be.

This is the first volume of **THE RISE OF LEGENDS, to the moon and beyond**!

Welcome to the Alphas.

> I will show you.
> I won't force you.
> But I won't wait for you.
> Dr. Bak Nguyen
> & William Bak

WILLIAM BAK

PAPA, J'SUIS PAS CON

CHAPTER 8
"PAPA, I'M NOT AN IDIOT"
by William Bak

This is the 3rd chapter of William's first solo book. The book was written in French to help him improve his French writing skills. I have translated for the occasion his words into Shakespeare's.

CHAPTER 3
"NO"
by William Bak

NO is a word that I use a lot. That is an understatement. I don't know why, but saying **NO** is so much easier than saying **YES**. Don't you think?

Once, my father asked me if I was in love with saying **NO**. I said **YES**. So, he started saying **NO** to everything, literally everything that I was asking. That sucked! It was only then that I realized how much I love to hear **YES**.

To be more specific, I love saying **NO** but I like to hear **YES**. My father told me that it does not make any sense. If I have said **NO** to him, well, he will respond with no too. That sounds just fair. In truth, that sucks! If I say **YES**, well, he will be doing the same.

Now you understand why it is so hard to say **NO** to my dad. Because if I am saying **NO**, I will also have to expect **NO**. So I start to say **YES**.

That's the general idea, but trust me, it is much harder to do than to say. The best example that comes to my mind is when it is about food. I love certain food like eggs, rice, and chicken. Those, I could eat all year long.

There are other things like radishes and lettuce which I can't stand. I tried and I hated the taste. Well, what do I respond to my father as he asks me to eat my vegetables? It is **YES** or **NO**?

I know what I really want to answer, but then, my father will be giving me the same answer every time that I will be asking for favours, like playing video games. Every time that I am saying **NO**, he will too! There are those days when my father is getting on my nerves!

Usually, at home, it is not that bad. I eat what I like. My parents and grandparents cook what they know I like to eat. The real problem occurs when we are travelling.

My parents love to travel, especially my mom. Well, while we are travelling, everything changes. My parents are not cooking and we often eat in restaurants. This is when it's getting complicated! I will be asking to eat at McDonald's and my father will answer with **YES**.

Then, we will all go to another restaurant, since my mom will not be eating McDonald's. My parents love to try and taste new things, especially when they travel. And guess what, they will try and they will be asking me to do the same! They will present me with weird kinds of food that I have never seen before. I don't want to put those in my mouth. So what do I answer? This is where I am trapped!

If I say **YES**, I will have to open my mouth and to try. If I say what is really on my mind, I will have to expect my dad to do the same. So what will happen the next time that I am hungry? He will say **NO** to McDonald's too!

Every time that I say **NO**, my life is getting complicated. Each time that I say **YES**, I have to do it and it is even more complicated! My father calls that being open. I try, I really do, but it so much harder than it is easier to say **YES**.

I guess, what I am trying to say is that saying **YES**, that's not always good. How many times, have I regretted trying new food. And each time, my father laughs with his hand on my shoulder telling me: "Well, now William, you at least know that you do not like!" What a joke! I knew that before even trying!

Some other times, it is not that bad. I did taste new food that I came to love. That's how I discover Greek pitas and Mexican tacos. Those are yummy!

In our books, we are saying that it is important to open our minds and our hearts. My father says that the easiest to open in our head is our mouth. I do not agree but what choice do I have? Each word has its consequence with my dad. That was me, younger.

Lately, a TV show changed my life. I am talking about Hell's Kitchen by Gordon Ramsay. I love that show, it is so entertaining. Me and my dad, we watch the show every time that we are eating. He too, loves the show.

We spent so much time watching Gordon Ramsay cook and fire other chefs. Eventually, it got to us and we started to understand the language of food and of cooking, sort to speak. Before, cooking was the realm of my mother.

Since Gordon Ramsay, my father started cooking. By cooking, I meant good food. I was the first one surprised. Since then, I am more and more open to trying and tasting new plates, especially as I heard so often words like Risotto and Beef Wellington! These too, I want to taste one day.

Thanks to Gordon Ramsay, I am now much more open to try new flavours. To be open starts with food but it does not stop there. When I start to say **YES**, I keep saying **YES**.

That's also true with **NO**. When I start with **NO**, more **NO**s are following. And by extension, I will also be hearing no more often. It's like Karma! On that, I am very happy to have discovered chef Ramsay and Hell's Kitchen.

> "MY FATHER OPENED MY MOUTH…
> MY MIND AND MY HEART FOLLOWED."
> **WILLIAM BAK**

Let's come back to travelling. I love to travel with my parents. Before, food was a big issue. I would say that we are resolving the situation since I discovered Gordon Ramsay. I am saying **YES** to try and then, if I don't like it, my parents never forced me to keep eating.

But as we are travelling, we have another problem. Often after days and days of walking, all that I want to do is to stay in the hotel room. It is luxurious and relaxing. But we did not travel that far to stay in the hotel, even if it is so nice! The goal to travel was to be able to see and to taste the world! That, my parents have been telling me very often.

I try to follow them as much as possible but if they were asking me, I would have stayed in the hotel. Of course, no one ever bothers to ask for my opinion! The truth is that I am too lazy to go out, to walk, and to try new food. But that is part of travelling, I learnt that through the years.

As I said, **NO** is a word that I like to say but not to hear. My father struggled with that too. To reset himself, he spent 18 months saying **YES** to literally everything and anything! I don't know how he survived that, but I can tell you that I liked him much better within that time. That was a great time for me!

I did ask him for toys and stuff but I never took advantage of the situation nor of his kindness. I love my dad dearly. What he learnt by saying **YES** to everything, he taught me. Especially with **YES** and **NO** and their consequences. You don't believe me? Am I not writing my first solo book?

I know that this is not helping my dad and his world record, but I also know how proud he is of me. Seriously, I never saw my dad that happy! He told me that this was the best gift anyone could have given him to celebrate his new landmark world record!

He will still have to correct and edit my book into **COMBO/ PAPERBACK** for Amazon and Apple. He will also have to produce an audiobook. Isn't that much work? My dad can be weird at times, I gave him more work and he is happy about that!!!

Me, I would have celebrated playing **PLAYSTATION** with my friends, but that's just me. I respect my dad and his choices. On top of dad, my dad is saying that he is lazy! I am lost, just completely lost. Thank you, papa!

My biggest problem with **YES** was about food. That has been resolved. I am not like my father, I can't say **YES** to everything. If you ask me, I think that there is a place for **YES** and one for **NO**. We just need to understand why.

I told that to my dad the other day. He answered with okay. I was surprised, I thought that I won and that was the end of my problems. Well, think again! The next time that I asked him to play **PLAYSTATION**, he asked me **WHY**?

> "WHY AND NO ARE ONE AND THE SAME.
> NO IS JUST QUICKER, THAT'S IT!"
> **WILLIAM BAK**

That put an end to my exploration on **WHY**. Now, it is **YES**, hoping that I would like or **NO**, knowing that I am closing myself down. I am maybe only 11-year-old, but I can tell you that every time that I closed myself down, I finished with regretting it dearly. And my dad will be there to remind me of my regrets! Haven't I told you how he could get on my nerves at times?

My name is William Bak, I love my life, I love my dad, and I love my mom. I love my 4 grand-parents and my uncles and ants too.

This is **PAPA, I AM NOT AN IDIOT**, the first solo book of William Bak. Welcome to the Alphas.

"Since I stopped saying NO, I stopped being an idiot."

WILLIAM BAK

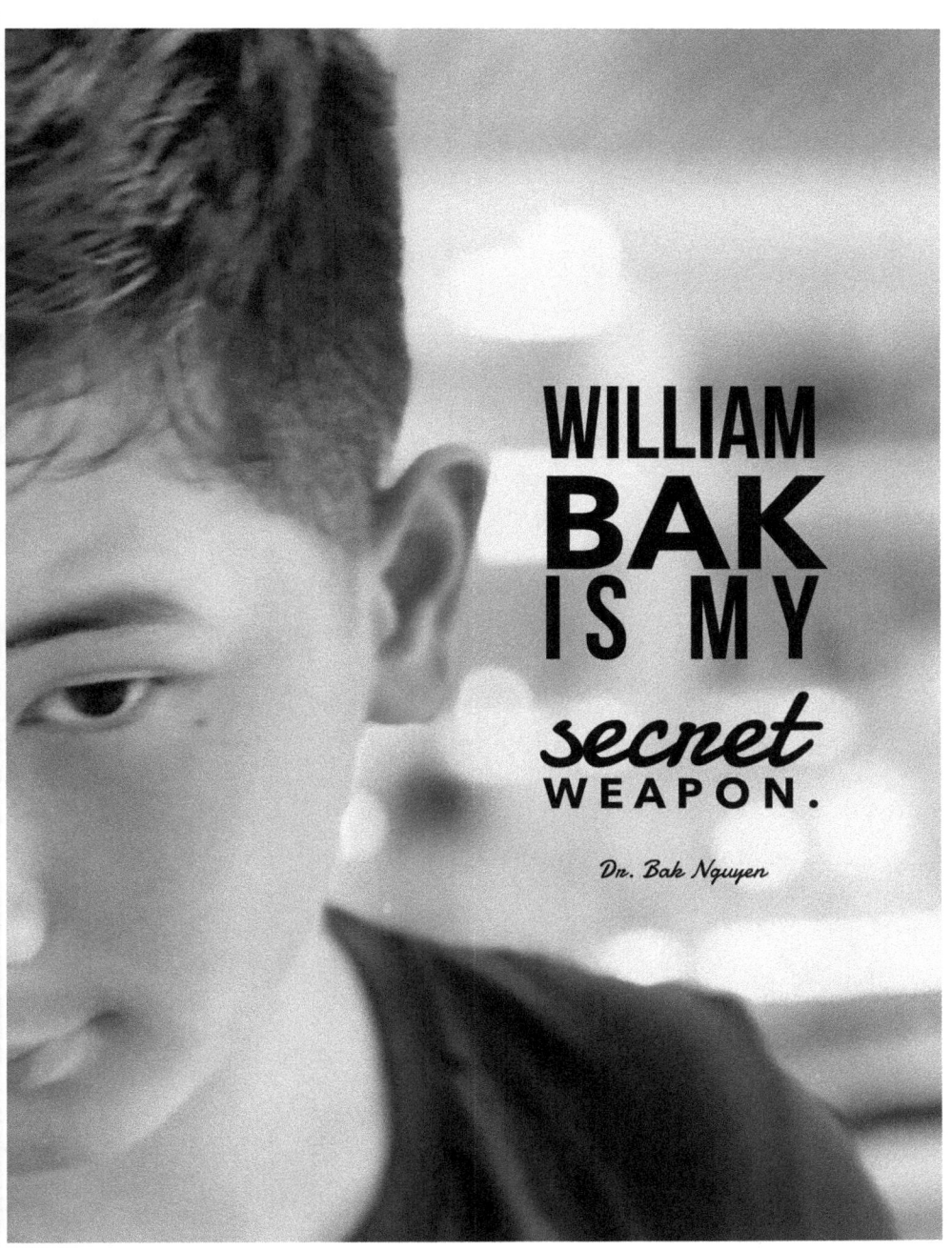

CHAPTER 9
"I BEAT MY DAD AT HIS OWN GAME"
by William Bak

Well, **PAPA, J'SUIS PAS CON**, is the first solo book that I wrote. It is also the only one so far. By the time of this writing, I am working on a 2nd solo book titled **ATTITUDE** or **ALTITUDE**, depending on how it goes.

> "TO GAIN ALTITUDE, DROP THE ATTITUDE."
> DR. BAK NGUYEN

Aren't you curious about why the title is not set yet? You will love that story. To know the insides and outs of that story, you will have to wait for me to finish that book, which will take the whole year, and wait for it to be available in the usual outlets. But trust me, that will be one worthy of your time!

Now, let's come back to my first solo book, **PAPA, J'SUIS PAS CON**. It was at the beginning of my last school year in elementary school. You know, at the beginning of each year, you take it slow and relax. Add to that, that I was starting in a new school. I didn't know many people and I needed to make new friends.

At school, I was busy making new friends. At home, it was pretty relaxed since it was the beginning of the year and the homework hasn't started yet. And then, my dad set his new landmark world record of writing 100 books in 4 years! That is huge!

I wanted to celebrate with him, but we are doing that every time that we finish a book together. This time, we needed something bigger, something bolder to celebrate his new landmark. I thought about what gift I could give him.

I was really looking to find something that would please my father. I thought about the books that I wrote. How many did I make? The funny thing is that I got lost in my thoughts and asked my dad how long did he take to write his first book. He said 14 days.

Lately, I am used to writing 300 words games' reviews to earn my playing time. So I asked him, if I write 1 chapter per day, knowing that we respect the number of the dragon which is 8, if I write 1 chapter a day, I would finish my book in 8 days, so beating him, right?

Hearing that, he smiled. His whole face was glowing. He told me that I still need an introduction and a conclusion. So that makes 10 days of writing, 300 words per day to beat my dad. Well, it was not that easy. He then told me that the minimum would be 500 words per chapter if I wanted a book. Without thinking further, I said deal!

I had a new challenge, one in which I could beat my father at his own game! I was ready to start right away, the idea of beating my dad was such a great motivation. But wait a minute, I still needed a subject to write about.

The era of the chickens was over. What else could I write about? It is then that my father reminded me that I wanted to write 2 books that famous night when I said I wanted to write books with him. The Lionheart became the Chickens books series. The other one was about me being a good son.

Well, this should be the perfect occasion to prove to my father how good of a son I am! So I started writing about what I knew best, my personal stories about living with my dad, THE Dr. Bak, and his world records.

I had so many things to say, and it would be easy since all I had to do was to tell stories from my memories. I was writing in French since I still needed to improve my writing skills to meet the French school standard. That was such a good start.

My father read the first chapter and he laughed so hard that he had tears in his eyes and pain in his stomach. I knew that I was on something great! Then he asked me about the title of my book. By then, I was calling it **THE GOOD SON**. That wasn't sexy at all, and I agreed.

We spent that evening fooling around with different titles to see what would stick. We decided to make it funny. How about playing with the concept of proving to my dad that I was not stupid? That is pretty much the same thing than saying that I am smart, but it would be funnier.

Oh, there is something that you have to know about my dad, he hates stupid! So the title became **PAPA, I'M NOT A IDIOT**, translation of **PAPA, J'SUIS PAS CON**. To tell you the truth, he was the one who arrived with the title. I simply loved the concept.

From being a good son to not being stupid, we totally changed gears and topics. But that title was very funny and was very intriguing to the readers. And just like that, it was decided that it will be my first solo book!

That did not help my dad with his world records and would be putting more work on his shoulders, but he was so happy! My dad could be strange at times!

So I put myself to work. 1 week of hard work, writing a chapter of 500 words a day for the following 10 days. I could do that. Just like my dad who wrote his books on top of being a CEO and a doctor, I wrote mine on top of school and my soccer practices.

To motivate me, my father gave me what I love the most. He brought me to TOYS R US, the giant toys store, and told me to choose my reward. We negotiated a little bit and he bought me 3 new Transformers!

I love Transformers. I was already pretty motivated to beat my dad, but now with Transformers on the line, I was pumped up! But to open them, I needed to finish the book within a week or so. I got back home and worked on my next chapter.

At some point, I set up the new unopened Transformers on my desk to keep my focus and motivation. Especially when I skipped a day writing because of soccer practice and had to make up for it, writing 2 chapters the next day.

That was not even the worst! The worst happened when I forgot to save one of my chapters and had to start over again! That was very, very frustrating!

"MY FATHER AND THE TRANSFORMERS GOT ME THROUGH!"
WILLIAM BAK

In the last days, my parents were going out with my grandparents. I stayed focused and brought my laptop to the mountain to write my chapter. We never foresaw that there would not be any internet connection up there and that WORDS won't be working without internet…

I brought my unopened Transformers with me and I found a way. I borrowed my father's iPhone and wrote with it. He told me that he too, wrote his first book from his phone! That was destiny, I was going through the same steps.

I finally wrote my last chapter, the conclusion by the 9th day. It was more night when I finished, but who cares, I did it! In 9 days, beating my father who wrote his in 14 days! I did it despite the setbacks and the fatigue. I was motivated!

To be honest, I was not tired at all that night! I was so happy to finally finish! I rewarded myself and opened all 3 of the Transformers. These, I earned with my words and my work. I also went online to play with my friends!

So what do I think of that whole experience? I am soooooooooooooooooooooooooo proud of myself to have beaten my father at his own game. Actually, he was as proud as I was! At the time, I was the happiest kid in the world.

For the next few weeks, I took some time off. But my father, being who he is, suggested that I could set another world record… and the story continues…

PAPA, J'SUIS PAS CON is the best and hardest book I wrote so far! I am very happy and proud to say that I beat, not only my father but the one and only Dr. Bak at his own game!

You all know how smart he is, and every time that we are playing a game together, he always wins! Not this time! This time, I beat him fair and square! It took me 11 years to beat my dad at his own game and I did it!

This is the first volume of **THE RISE OF LEGENDS, to the moon and beyond**!

Welcome to the Alphas.

I will show you.
I won't force you.
But I won't wait for you.
Dr. Bak Nguyen
& William Bak

> Travelling is the best way to keep your heart and mind open. It should be mandatory to travel once or twice a year!
>
> DR. BAK NGUYEN

CHAPTER 10
"TRIBUTES"
by Dr. Bak Nguyen

We surfed for a long moment on the last achieved victories, my landmark world record and William's first solo book. That overwhelmed all of my emotional systems. So instead of slowing down, I speeded up my momentum to the next level. Before the end of September, we wrote **PROLOGUES OF DESTINY**, published the **COMBO paperback/audiobook** and by October, you could hear it on streaming, **UAX** version.

Yes, we were once more in momentum. We were still in COVID but our morale was through the roof. On the company side, Mdex was preparing to open its first expansion since COVID. That was a huge win too!

We went to Toronto to celebrate all of these victories and to shoot the videos for the launch of **PROLOGUES OF DESTINY** and interviews of my latest landmark world record. Well, we were so busy that it took us until Canadian Thanksgiving before we could celebrate our victories. On the top of the CN Tower, we, Tranie, William, and I, celebrated our hard-earned victories.

> "IF YOU ARE JUMPING FROM WIN TO WIN, YOU MUST ALSO CELEBRATE EACH SINGLE VICTORY, NO MATTER HOW BIG OR HOW SMALL."
> DR. BAK NGUYEN

Then, an officer of Mdex lost both his parents within the following weeks. We were devastated for him. He lost both his parents within 7 days. I helped him with his speech.

Helping him to write these words of farewell to his mother, I realized that I don't want to do that when my parents won't be around to listen to my thoughts.

That pushed me to write: **L'art de transformer de la soupe en magie**, a tribute to my dear mother. That became book #103. Then, it was close to the Holidays season and my father was next in line.

William wanted to join me on that tribute to my dad. We created **AU PAYS DES PAPAS**. Yes, those 2 were in French because my parents read more French than English.

Just like with **LEGENDS OF DESTINY**, we created different characters to populate our narrative. Well, writing about my father is very tricky, to say the least. My father likes the praises, who doesn't, but he is a very, very private person. He saw the book I dedicated to my mother and he would have been upset if I did not have anything coming up for him.

That said, now that he knew that a book was coming for his homage, he was very embarrassed to say the less. He was very uneasy. To him, writing a book is like going to the confessional and telling the world, your sins. He shared his thoughts with me by December that year.

We were about halfway through the writing of his homage, writing, audiobook, and UAX album, all in parallel. Those were supposed to be his Christmas gift. That cut short our momentum, to William and I.

We are left hanging, not knowing how to spin that one. We were too advanced to cancel that book, and yet, we lost our main spine, motivation, and narrative all at once.

Last Christmas, we were in a void of creativity. This year was going in the same direction, only this time, it wasn't William's fault. My father never understood what he's just done to us, and that, he will never know. We both respected his privacy and wish.

4 months went by before we could find the motivation and the inspiration to spin **AU PAYS DES PAPAS** into a book that we would be proud of, one not infringing on my father's wishes.

I brought back the focus of the story on William and on myself, looking for the recipe to make the perfect dad. We changed elements here and there and developed the characters into unique heroes.

We discussed the storyline together. Then, William had to write the 500 words chapters. I would take over from there to write the final version making it into our book. Well, by Spring that year, we signed **AU PAYS DES PAPAS 1**.

When we first had the idea of **AU PAYS DES PAPAS**, there were 2 volumes planned for that franchise. Well, after being torpedoed by my father that Christmas, we both concluded that we would stop at one.

Then, following our own mentality of celebration, we went to New York to record the launch of that book, **AU PAYS DES PAPAS**.

This is the first volume of **THE RISE OF LEGENDS, to the moon and beyond**!

Welcome to the Alphas.

I will show you.
I won't force you.
But I won't wait for you.
Dr. Bak Nguyen
& William Bak

CHAPTER 11
"PAPALAND"
by Dr. Bak Nguyen & William Bak

Here is the first chapter of **PAPALAND**, the English title to **AU PAYS DES PAPAS**, after revision and reedition to respect my father's privacy. William and I spent much time and energy to make this one work.

I have translated the next chapter from French into English. We hope that you will enjoy it.

EPISODE 1
"THE CHRISTMAS TALES"
by Dr. Bak Nguyen & William Bak

It is on a beautiful sunny December morning that William wakes up. As soon as he opened his eyes, Hush jumps on his bed to greet him good morning by generously licking his face. That's always a good way to wake up.

Today is Saturday, there is no school! This is what is so great about weekends, no school! William runs to the window and sees snowflakes dancing in the wind. It's going to be a wonderful day! He got dressed and runs to his parents to greet them good morning!

- Good morning, Master William.
- Good morning Paul.

Right outside his bedroom, the butler smiled as he watched William jumping with great enthusiasm out of his bed. He runs to his parent's room. Hush follows him, barking happily.

There is a long hallway separating William's bedroom from his parent's. As he keeps running, he passes the household staff who all wish him: "Good morning Master William." The last person to greet him is Edith, his governess. She smiles gently at him, and winks to remind him to brush his teeth first!

His father never passes up an opportunity to remind him to brush his teeth! William slows down abruptly to change direction for the bathroom.

Behind him, Hush tries to change direction just as quickly, but the marble floor is so slippery that she skids into the wall and hits her head. That was a small bump with no consequence. She resumes her race to join William.

He brushes his teeth and is ready to start this wonderful new day with his parents. He cleans his teeth and his hair, with Edith's help. Now, he is ready to greet his parents.

- Good morning Papa! Good morning Mama!

His voice echoes in an empty room. Before the cold and sadness invades his heart, Hush warms the room, making cheerful noises. Edith is right behind. With a maternal hand, she hugs William.

- Are you hungry? Paul made pancakes in the kitchen, just for you!

William's parents are often gone on business trips. They were supposed to come back last night but a storm delayed their flight. William wanted to stay up to welcome them, but Edith insisted that Master William be in bed before 10 PM.

- A storm delayed their plane, they will be here later tonight.
- ...

This is nothing new. William is used to this song: a big house, lots of toys, Paul and Edith to keep him company, and all of Hush's love. And yet, William would have given so much to spend more time with his parents, especially his father.

William finishes his breakfast alone, with Hush at his feet. Just when he thinks the day has started badly, he hears a very familiar voice behind him:

- Where is my favourite grandson?

It's Grandpa! Both Hush and William run to throw themselves into Grandpa's arms! Grandpa knows that Mom and Dad have been delayed, but he didn't come for them, he came to see William.

- Today, we're going to get your Christmas present, okay?
- This year, I don't want toys. My father promised to write a book with me. This will be my Christmas gift for this year!
- Wow, you are going to write a book! For that, you will need a beautiful manuscript to write your stories! Let's get you the most beautiful notebook, one with a nice leather cover.
- One with a padlock on the cover like in Goosebumps?
- Sure, why not? But I hope you will be writing great stories, not ghost stories!
- That, I promise you, Grandpa.

The bookstore was packed with people. The store was so packed that people were lining up at the doors just to get in. If you think that the line to get in was bad, the lines at the cashiers were even worse. Grandpa was ready to wait, but it was cold and William didn't want Grandpa to catch a cold.

They finally decided to go to the small store across the street, a small antique and souvenir shop. Unlike the big bookstore, there was no one in that shop.

A bell hanging on the door announced the arrival of William, Hush, and Grandpa. At the cashier, an old grumpy man with glasses too heavy for his nose did not even look up to greet them. It felt like in these classic Christmas ghost stories.

- Please, sir, do you have any blank books?
- Blank books? For that, go get them in the superstore across the street. Here, our books are not empty!
- I beg your pardon, begins Grandpa. He meant books in which he can write.

- We only sell treasures here sir, not colouring books.

Grandpa smiles at the grumpy old man. Meanwhile, William wanders the very tight aisles of the store, looking for a book with a padlock on the cover.

Everything is upside down in the store. There are so many old things for sale that William doesn't know where to even start looking. It is very different from the large bookstore across the street with its large and orderly shelves and sections.

Grandpa joins William, making his way across the books and antiques. He finally reaches William and kneels down to talk with his grandson at eye level.

Grandpa always does that, he makes William feel like the most important person in the whole world, unlike the other adults who talk down on him.

- Did you find anything?
- Not yet Grandpa, there are so many things here. I can't find anything and I do not dare to touch anything either. The old man in front scares me a little.

At these words, Grandpa starts laughing.

- The old gentleman is very serious, but he is not mean.

As Grandpa and William were talking, Hush found something. She calls them over, of course, barking. It is an old book, with a leather cover and a padlock. The book was on the ground, buried under a mountain of old newspapers. Grandpa saw it too, he helps William with the newspapers and pulls out the old book.

There is a broken padlock on the cover that wouldn't close. Inside, there are no white sheets to write on, the pages are all yellow, but you could write inside since the aged pages have faded away all the words printed before.

- **Yes, that's it! I want that one! It's really like in the movies!**

With these words, Grandpa got up, smiled with a gentleman's confidence, and walked toward the grumpy old man to negotiate. William did not know how much Grandpa paid for that book, but it was truly a magical gift. And it was Hush who found it!

***

Once upon a time, there was a father, a son, and a mother. They were not rich, but they were happy. They lived in a small cabin in the woods. If the other children had gifts and toys for Christmas, Guillaume had his mom and dad.

Every year, Christmas lasts for the whole 2 weeks of the holiday break! No school and just magic! The entire 14 days were spent decorating the house, baking muffins, and listening to stories around the fire. Only for these 14 days, Guillaume could sleep with Mom and Dad! That, we must not say too loudly, it would be embarrassing if the other children found out.

That morning, Guillaume got up and ran towards the window. A beautiful white day was defining in front of his eyes. Today will be the day to find his perfect Christmas tree with his dad.

No, they won't go to the store, but they will walk through the woods and find the perfect tree for this year. Every year, it's a magical moment between dad and son.

After eating all his Mom's breakfast, Guillaume dressed warmly for the big day. As he opened the door, he could feel the magic and the winter wind caressing his face. Quickly, Hush ran out into the snow.

There was so much snow that Hush was completely submerged under the snow. You can't see her, but you can follow her movements underneath the white blanket...

Papa came out and took Guillaume on his shoulders in search of the magic tree. Their small hut stood on a tiny hill. Just a few minutes away, there was a very dense wooded area.

A few minutes away, that's walking by summertime. In winter, it takes so much longer to walk through the snow. Not for Hush, she always ran as fast, summer and winter, snow or not.

Every year, it is Guillaume who finds the magic tree. This year, he can't find any. There are fir trees everywhere, but none are magical. His father is a very patient man, he woke the whole forest waiting for Guillaume to make his pick.

The sun began to set and still no magic tree yet. Guillaume must now walk, his father is too tired to carry him. Papa looks at Guillaume and asks him to choose one, anyone.

- **I don't know Papa. I don't see anything magical this year.**

Papa was growing impatient facing Guillaume's lack of decision, but he kept smiling to not spoil the magic of the day. It is finally Hush who will have chosen the magic tree of this year... she found it *marking* her territory.

Papa and Guillaume both agreed, Hush found the magic tree. It's just that the tree was gigantic, at least twice as big as the one they would normally choose. We don't negotiate magic! Papa took out his saw and got to work.

The tree is so big that it took the rest of the day to cut it down and bring it home. Papa is strong, but the tree that Hush chose was really, really big.

When they finally got home, it was already dark. Mom was waiting at the window. She had cooked a hot stew to welcome the return of her men and Hush. Guillaume ran into the kitchen and Hush got ahead of him. It was just Dad who stayed behind with the magic tree... it was too big to fit through the door! The tree, not Papa...

Papa always finds a solution.

Guillaume woke up in the middle of the night, still fully dressed. In the living room, the magnificent magic tree was fully decorated. Yesterday, he was so tired, that he fell asleep on the dining table while he was finishing his stew.

His mom and dad brought in the magic tree in a very creative and clever way. Guillaume could see the branches glued and taped back together using adhesive tape. Mom used the garlands to cover the joints, and Papa hid them behind the big ornaments.

Papa had to cut and rebuild the tree, once passed the door! And Hush? She's sleeping under the tree...

***

- No, no, and no, this is getting nowhere Papa. It's not funny and it's too slow!
- You are right William. Have we lost it? Have we lost our inspiration? It's been two beginnings that we've thrown away.
- Yes Papa, we were better with chickens! That was our thing! I'm hungry, are you?

For 4 years now, the Christmas tradition has been to eat popcorn, build replica models and watch movies. Last year, William and his father built the Hogwarts Castle in Harry Potter and went through the marathon of the 8 movies of the series. That, and writing new books together.

For the previous years, that was fun, but that was not enough for this year...

- Let's eat and we'll catch up tomorrow, after a good night's sleep.
- But Papa, aren't we going to visit Grandma and Grandpa tomorrow?
- Oh, I forgot about that! With the Christmas holidays, I lost count. Thank you William. Let's start by eating. What did mom cook for us?

This is William's great life in the Mdex Mansion, an extravagant life with his parents, the magic of the chickens, the legends, his Papa, and this breakdown of inspiration.

The next day was family day. The whole family went to visit William's Grandparents. Every year, around this time, Grandma is always sad. It reminds her how much she misses Hush, her little dog. Hush was Grandma's best friend for over 10 years. Grandpa loved her too.

Grandpa and Grandma are from another era. They don't cry, they rarely show emotions, but you can feel their sadness, especially Grandma's. William too, misses Hush very, very much.

To lighten the mood, William asked to push Grandma's wheelchair to spend some quality time alone with her. After the brunch, he pushed Grandma for a quick walk in the park. It wasn't too cold and the white snowflakes wiped away Grandma's invisible tears.

William was very attentive to the emotional charge and the vibe. He stayed silent. He put his hand on Grandma's shoulder to say her that he was there with her. She felt all of his love and warmth. William was his favourite grandson! In fact, William is her only grandson!

After the walk, they went home. On the ride home, there was tension between Grandpa and Papa. There was no argument, no one even said a word, but everyone could feel the heaviness and the cold, not of winter, but of their dispute. William never knows how to react in such moments. Over time, he learnt to stay silent, waiting for the storm to pass.

Why is Grandpa often grumpy? William knew better, he had to save this question for later, but why? It's Christmas after all! Why did it feel like walking on eggshells? He saw his dad's mood darken more and more.

Papa tried to keep his humour, but he doesn't laugh as naturally anymore. Mom stood silent, almost distant. She knew better than to get involved in these situations. They drove Grandpa and Grandma home.

It will surely take a few hours, but that will pass too. Papa always ends up with his gorgeous smile back. He is built like that, it is stronger than him, the joy always resurfaces, sooner or later. And when joy returns, William will be there to welcome his dad!

At home, William approached his Dad and hugged him gently. He wanted his daddy to know how much he loves him. And the lack of inspiration?

- Papa?
- Yes, William?
- I wanted to ask you, why Grandpa is often so grumpy, but along the way, I had a new idea.
- Really? What is your new idea?
- Why don't we write a book on the recipe to be the Perfect Father? Maybe it will help Grandpa?
- ... that's an idea William. You will then have to convince Grandpa to read it...

Before he even finished his sentence, Papa started laughing. Very quickly, William joined him. William has the magic gift: to make people laugh, especially to make his dad laugh. Mom looked at William as the champion of the day, he brought back the joy and magic of Christmas!

- The recipe to be the Perfect Father... I like it! William, shall we start tonight?
- Tonight Papa? But you promised that I could play video games...
- Okay. How about tomorrow morning?
- That's a deal! Thank you Papa and merry Christmas!
- Merry Christmas? Christmas is only in 5 days!
- Since I do not have school, every day is Christmas to me! Merry Christmas Papa!
- I see, you picked that up from Guillaume. These stories were not a complete waste of time after all...

William spent the evening playing until 10PM. At 10 sharp, he stopped playing and went to kiss Mom and Dad good night.

- Papa, can I sleep with you? Just for the holidays? Please, please?

- Nice try William, do you really want your friends to know that you slept with your parents this holiday?

And everyone, William, Mama, and Papa, all laughed to tears. That night was a great night's sleep for William, the hero who saved the day. Dr. Bak found his joy, and Mom was more than happy to see both her men happy.

By the next morning, as promised, William was up at 8 AM to start the book on the recipe to be the Perfect Father. He found his father already at his desk. His father was speechless. William approached without really knowing what is going on.

On the table, he saw a book, an old book with a leather cover and a broken padlock on it.

- Stop kidding Papa! This is it! How did you manage to find the same book as in our story?
- I didn't. I thought it was you and Mom who wanted to surprise me!
- Stop teasing me Papa, I'm not stupid, remember? Shall we start?

William sat at the desk, next to his father. Dr. Bak shrugs and laughs, this time William and his mom really pulled magic from their bag of tricks! It is Christmas after all! Time for real magic! That's better than a Christmas tree!

Dr. Bak opened the book. The pages are yellowed, dusty, and empty. To tell you the truth, Dr. Bak does not write in a book, he writes on his computer. But let's keep an open mind!

William thought that it was really cool to write in an old manuscript, exactly like in the movies! He picked up a pencil and began to write on the first page: The Recipe to be the Perfect Father, by Dr. Bak and William Bak.

- Papa, why is it that your name always comes first?
- If you write the whole book while I speak, you can have your name before mine!
- No thanks, that's not a good deal!

And of course, both of them, to their heart's delight, laughed again. Laughter is the language that made the connection between father and son so magical. Dr. Bak, at his turn, picked up the pencil and wrote: EPISODE 1.

- William, are we writing chapters or episodes?
- Do you want to write a cookbook or a movie? Me, I prefer a movie. Fewer and fewer people are reading anyway.
- That is sad, but you are right! So let's write episodes, that would be more fun!

As Dr. Bak and William returned to the book to write their first words, they found an empty book with many yellow pages. It seemed that all the previous words got erased or faded away with time. That was intriguing! They carefully examine the book… the magic book.

Dr. Bak picked up the old book and went through all the pages. He held the book a little too close and as the pages were flipping, a small cloud of dust awoke his allergies. He sneezed. With that blow, an even bigger cloud of dust arose from the pages of the old book.

The cloud of dust filled out the huge hall in which Dr. Bak's office was located. The dust was so thick and dense that they couldn't see each other anymore.

- **Stop it Papa, it's not funny anymore!**
- **William, you really have to tell me where you and your mom found such great movie props! The effects are amazing!**

At these words, Dr. Bak sneezed again, but this time much harder. The cloud of dust eventually dissipates, making way for the birds of the forest who began to sing...

This is **PAPALAND.** Welcome to the Alphas.

Dr. BAK NGUYEN
& WILLIAM BAK

CHAPTER 12
"WE ARE NOT GIVING UP"
by Dr. Bak Nguyen & William Bak

AU PAYS DES PAPAS, in English, is **PAPALAND**. I know, it sounds weird in English, that's why we wrote the book in French. Actually, there is a legacy reason why French was our language of choice for that one. It was supposed to be a tribute to my grandpa, and since my grandpa reads more French than English, we chose his language.

That turned out to be a big miss when a few weeks later, he told my father that he does not want to have a public homage. My dad respected his privacy and we were stuck with half of a book that did not make sense anymore.

It took us a few months to fix but we will come back to that later. Well, we fixed the storyline and the characters to respect the privacy of my grandpa, but the legacy of that was that French stayed for that book.

The other reason why we made this one in French is because of me. I am getting better in French at school and I wanted to keep improving. To be honest, I now prefer to write in French. **AU PAYS DES PAPAS** is one of my best books!

That all started after my father finished writing a book as a tribute to my grandma. After that, he wanted to honour his dad and recruited me for the occasion. I always say yes to my dad. One, because I love him, and two, because we are partners. Writing books together, as father and son, was fun, until it became family stuff, loaded with family drama. After that my grandpa basically shot us down with his wish for privacy, my father was demolished. He then put me in charge to continue the book.

It was Christmas in COVID and we were stuck with a dead-end book with no motivation. We celebrated Christmas with very few people, having only my parents and grandparents. The magic was hard to ignite. On the book front, we were stuck in neutral. For months! It took 4 more months to find the courage and inspiration to make this one work. And it does not mean that we did not try. I wrote a few chapters but they were horrible. My father did his best but couldn't save them. We restarted a few times.

Nothing is better to kill the vibe than to have to rewrite a chapter! That will kill motivation, inspiration, and vibe all at once. Our problem was that our story had no more direction after that we took my grandpa out of the story.

It is finally when we decided to refocus the story around me and my dad that it started to make sense again. We got inspired to write the PAPAS as if they were SMURFS. To do that, we had to redraft our characters and develop their personality. We spent a few evenings making jokes and laughing as we were creating the PAPAS. They are basically caricatures of Dads we met in real life. Not just my grandpa, but my father's and other fathers' too.

Because it was not about my grandpa, we could be as mean as we wanted. The meaner we get with the PAPAS personalities and attitudes, the funnier it got. This is when the magic started to come back.

It is basically about me and my dad waking up in a dream in **PAPALAND**. Hush, the dog of my grandma was brought back as a tribute too. We never got to say goodbye to Hush when she died. This was our way to rewrite that story too.

In **PAPALAND**, we are stuck. All that I want is to come back home. But not my dad, he thinks that it is funny and, since it is a dream, he does not take anything seriously. I was left, in the story, to be the adult for the both of us.

If that would happen in real life, I am sure that it would not be funny, but not at all. But since that happened in our story, my imaginary self was so frustrated while me and my dad were laughing the whole time that we wrote the story. Then, we met with the PAPAS!

I wrote chapters of 500 words, one every 2 to 3 days. I still had school, homework, and exams to prepare for. Then, it was about not 5 PAPAS but a whole city of PAPAS. We started with a village but that quickly grew into a hidden city underground after the reboot (after we recuperated from my grandpa's torpedoes).

Actually, the village was just a cover for the underground city. Doing so, no one could ever accuse us of copying the SMURFS. That was our inspiration but we grew it into our own fantasy world.

Imagine that you sleep and you wake up in a fantasy land, stuck with ridiculous PAPAS to bother you! That was basically the script of our renewed book. We included more and more jokes in the dialogue and the script. What started as a pain in the butt became so entertaining, funny, and fun to work on. Then, we carried on.

Our conclusion was so good that neither me nor my dad were ready to let go yet. Don't get me wrong, the torpedoes traumatized both of us and we concluded that we would only write one book of **PAPALAND**.

After the completion of **PAPALAND**, we went to New York to celebrate. We shot videos and interviews and had much fun telling the story of how we made that book.

In New York, we were walking the city and what happened to me in the book happened to me in real life too! Not to the exact details, but that was close enough! I won't spoil the book here, but if you want to know, what happened to me in chapter

2 of **PAPALAND**, happened to me in real life as I was in New York.

In the book, my dad was laughing the whole way through. Well, in real life, he was laughing too! Maybe not as hard but he had the time of his life. I wasn't sharing the same perspective, but I ended up laughing eventually. Well, we were so into it that, I don't really remember exactly how, but we got sucked back into it and decided to write a 2nd volume to the story.

This book is maybe the most complex story structure that I wrote so far. I wrote every chapter, 500 words each time. Looking back, I am proud and hopeful to see my **children** (books) grow into maybe movies eventually!

PAPALAND was, by far, the funniest book that we ever wrote until that point. I am surprised and happy to see that it became a huge success and how funny it turned out to be. I am proud but also sad to see how long it took us to write something that good!

This is the first volume of **THE RISE OF LEGENDS, to the moon and beyond**!

Welcome to the Alphas.

I will show you.
I won't force you.
But I won't wait for you.
Dr. Bak Nguyen
& William Bak

CHAPTER 13
" THE GAMES AND THE ELVES"
by Dr. Bak Nguyen

The torpedoes that my father aimed at us, without him knowing, sunk our inspiration for months. William and I were not sure how to salvage our ship of **PAPALAND**.

We did not stop at that, we went back to the **LEGENDS OF DESTINY**, editing the promotional videos we shot last fall as we were in Toronto. Talking about the gods, the angels, the elves, and the demons got us back into momentum.

We decided to start the second volume of the series, with **THE BOOK OF ELVES**. For that book, I needed a clear distraction from the torpedoes and the sunken ship, so we went all-in on fun. I spent evenings and evenings with William, playing Starcraft 2.

It was surely very distracting and entertaining. What is very special about Starcraft 2 is that it is a team strategy game and just like a sport, we have access to replays to study our best moves and our worst. Well, we watched our replay to get better, as a team, but that led us to a fortunate discovery.

Watching the replay, we had the chance to follow our soldiers and workers, one by one, and how they survived, or not, our orders. Zooming now on the first-person point of view, we just found new ways to tell our stories. And this is how we wrote the second volume of **LEGENDS OF DESTINY**.

We had the macro storyline in mind, but thanks to Starcraft 2, we now have a way to approach the storytelling from the ground, from the perspective of the heroes fighting, bleeding, and dying on the battlefield. That added such realistic and organic layers to our stories. Within weeks, **THE BOOKS OF ELVES** was completed.

That was such a relief, both of us were traumatized by last year's shortage of inspiration. And what about the **UAX** album? That too was in our minds. But then, I hit a wall. I was exhausted.

For now months, years, I was running a marathon of sprints, setting new world records and landmark world records. I invented new styles and media and got the industry to accept them. I was fighting COVID from a health worker's standpoint and bearing the weight of the Pandemic on my entrepreneurial shoulders. Suddenly, I felt so tired, almost hopeless.

> "IT WAS LIKE MY BODY WAS SO EXHAUSTED THAT AS SOON AS MY MIND SLOWED DOWN, EVERYTHING STARTED TO BREAK DOWN."
> DR. BAK NGUYEN

Physically, I was doing fine, except that I gained so much weight. I was always tired, and now I was getting more and more grumpy. My patience was running thinner and thinner. I was becoming a bomb waiting to explode at any moment.

Tranie was exhausted too but she was still in control. She forced the whole family to take a time off in the Dominican Republic, now that it was permitted to travel the world. She did not have to make her case for long.

More than ever, we all needed these vacations and, I believed, earned them without the shadow of a doubt. Actually, I think that everyone who went through the last 2 years of Pandemic, earned their vacations. This is bigger than to rest and to relax. It is about mental health.

> **"TRAVELLING IS THE BEST WAY TO KEEP YOUR HEART AND MIND OPEN. IT SHOULD BE MANDATORY TO TRAVEL ONCE OR TWICE A YEAR!"**
> DR. BAK NGUYEN

After a few nights and days of sleeping and resting, I was back on track with William. We took advantage of the wonderful sun and the magical vibe of the 5 stars resort for the background of our next video, the official launch of **PAPA, J'SUIS PAS CON**, on COMBO paperback/audiobook on Amazon, on e-book on Kindle and Apple Books. Recently, it has also been accepted by Audible, the biggest distributor of audiobooks to join their library.

From a family's well-deserved vacations, it became the stage of our new celebrations. We shot, edited, have much fun, and sleep. And the **UAX** album of **THE BOOK OF ELVES**?

That is still on my to-do list since the last few months. I got Amazon, Apple Books, and Audible to distribute that one. I promise you that sooner or later, it will also make it into streaming, **UAX** version, on Apple Music, Spotify, Amazon Prime, and the other major music platforms too. The only question is when.

This is the first volume of **THE RISE OF LEGENDS, to the moon and beyond**!

Welcome to the Alphas.

I will show you.
I won't force you.
But I won't wait for you.
Dr. Bak Nguyen
& William Bak

CHAPTER 14
" THE BOOK OF ELVES"
by Dr. Bak Nguyen & William Bak

Here's one chapter of **THE BOOK OF ELVES**. Since this book is a much elaborated storyline, it wasn't easy to sample out one chapter to give you a taste of the action. I narrowed it down to the one most influenced by our new way of telling the story.

William and I really hope that you will enjoy your reading.

Chapter 4
Mildor's Gate

by Dr. Bak Nguyen & William Bak

Since they went back to their old ways and left the technology and all the craziness behind, the elves, now known as the dark elves are retreating to the forest and the undeveloped parts of Destiny, to live as their ancestors once did.

The Shamans are back in power and magic is once more, the beating heart of the tribes. Far in the North East, one of the dark tribe settlements recruits many of the unsatisfied Elves of the close by Metropolis. They cut all communication with the Metropolis, networking only amongst dark tribes.

The North-East tribe was under the leadership of Shaman Ivaran Faedan. Even if there were 2 other counsellors, Shaman Ivaran was the one in power. He and his tribe fortified the North Gates, colonizing the Northern old forest. To the South was the 5th Metropolis and to the North was a chain of mountains making a natural wall against any invaders.

Beyond the chain of mountains, they are lava lands, as they called them, swamps heated up by the underground volcanoes. These lands were worthless. Basically, there were very few openings in the chain of mountains to access these lava lands. The biggest passage was through a narrow corridor where 2 of the mountains met. They call that corridor, the Mildor's Gate.

Shaman Ivaran had 3 outposts built at the passage, calling them the Mildor's Gate. They were guarded by dark Elves employing magic, cloak, and arrows to protect their land. All of these Elves were female warriors.

For decades, they guarded the Gates without any incident but savage creatures looking for a meal. What is special about these creatures was their size: they were gigantic: giant spiders, giant wolves, giant snakes, even dragons.

Most of the trespassers were simply put down by the dark warriors of the outposts. Eventually, they evolved and captured some specimens and domesticated them. Giant wolves became the rides of these female elves' warriors.

The rumours that flying dragons were seen beyond the horizon of the chain of mountains fed the imagination of the nostalgics. Since they were back to the old elf's ways, the idea of resurrecting the Knights Order was very popular, especially within the Northern tribes.

The warriors trained since their childhood and a new generation of Knights were ready to be reborn. They still needed their ride, the dragons mounted by their ancestors. Dragons went extinct after the last volcano eruptions that cleansed a fifth of Destiny. Now, with these rumours, it was a sign of the Gods, that Elf glory will rise once again.

Quickly, the outposts in the Mildor's Gate saw more and more dragons hunters. They stop at the gate only to begin their quest, beyond the wall. No one has ever come back with a dragon yet. But they all came back. Until that day, 3 hunters went for their hunt with big hopes. Only one came back, barely holding his limps together: the Orcs were invading!

The regiment of Elves took the menace very seriously and sent out for help and reinforcement. They stood on high alert for the whole night. Nothing. By morning, reports from the eastern outpost came in as they were attacked by 2 single Orc warriors, a giant male, and a cloaked female. These 2 killed most of the garrison stationed there, and the few survivors were the ones bringing the news of the attack.

Everyone was on high alert, war has started once more with the Orcs. They were scouting the horizon, ready to shoot and kill whatever shape appeared in front of their eyes. They saw more dark elves running back. They were from the northwest outpost. That post had fallen too. The same story was reported: 2 single warriors, a giant male Orc, and an invisible female Orc wiped out their garrison.

A few days later, when the reinforcement arrived from the tribe, all 3 outposts were burned to the ground. No one survived but those fleeing with the wounded before the attack.

Shaman Ivaran came himself. With his own eyes, he witnessed death and destruction. By now, the whispers were about an army of ghost Orc assassins. He was left with no choice but to evacuate his tribe and alert the Elves of the Metropolis, asking for help and protection.

***

The rumours were all true. Delmott and Durz went up to scout the native Elves' defenses. Since there were so under guarded, they wiped them out, leaving no witnesses. Because they were only 2, some fled successfully.

Delmott was very aware that this meant war but better to blow the first strike than to be caught by the rising lava. For all of his life, he prepared for this day. For all of his life, he was afraid of this day. Preemptive and surgical strike, that was his plan.

While he and Durz cleaned the way, Smogulg organized the migration of the whole herd. They went up and settled temporarily North of the chain of mountains, closer to the heat of the swamp. If the lava does not rise any higher, they could soon return home.

***

Elves scouts reported the new settlements of the invading Orc army, counting thousands of arrivals. The war has started. The Elves

Council quickly dispatched 2 captains with their regiment to reinforce Mildor's Gate. With the growing number of the Orc army and the number of fleeing Elves population, their mission was first and foremost to hold the Gate and to stall for long enough to evacuate the local population.

Even if the 2 regiments sent were powerful, they might not be enough to face a full-scale war. Reinforcement and air support will be sent by the other 7 Metropolis. Their orders were to hold the ground until reinforcement came.

Ehrendil Miadi and Klaudel Miralynn were the 2 captains. Ehrendil was more of hot blood and the hero type, charging head down first. Klaudel was more the thinker and calculus type. They did not like each other much. Although of the same rank, Ehrendil took the lead with his troops and arrived first on the ground. Klaudel, more organized, arrived after.

Because of that, most warriors looked up to Ehrendil as the commander and Klaudel as the supporting officer. That just spread more animosity between the 2 captains. They went in with troops and weapons and with engineers too. They had to rebuild and fortify the gate. This time, the Orcs will be met with energy blasters, not cloaked arrows.

Adamar Daralei is an engineer serving under Captain Ehrendil. He was posted on the forefront of the Gate with the mission to rebuild the East and North Outposts. Adamar is also one of Zeno's 7 adopted sons. All of his life, he was disregarded by his siblings because he wasn't as creative. Adamar never invented anything. He was just very quick in redoing the blueprints of others. He went to live in the 5th Metropolis to escape family pressure.

Little did he know that he would be the first one to be called on duty. Actually, he kept his family ties very discreet. His commander never knew that a son of the supreme counsellor was serving under him.

Ehrendil was very ambitious and impatient. The elves called him passionate. He was the hero type and was loved as such. After burying the bodies of the fallen regiments, Ehrendil refused to clean the blood and soil from his hands and inspired his warriors to make the Orc pay for each drop of Elf blood spilled. They are rallied behind him.

So he charged head down with his Elves, despite the protests of Klaudel and the orders received from the Council. Klaudel held on to his troops and fortified his position while Ehrendil led the charge against the Orc army, without any reinforcement.

Ehrendil is a very skilled and powerful warrior but so were the Orcs he met in combat. One after the next, he saw his warriors killed. At each death, Ehrendil doubled down on his rage to kill the enemy. He was a beast who did not care who was getting hurt. The Orcs noticed that and so had the Elves following him. Despite the odds and the death count rising, Ehrendil kept pushing into Orc territories.

The way was cleared for Klaudel's troops to arrive and swap the victory but Klaudel and his troops stayed behind in their fortified position. Technically, Klaudel was following the orders in hand.

That infuriated Ehrendil who went mad and drove all of his troops for a final blow, meeting on the battlefield, Delmott himself. Adamar was posted as a supporting engineer, deep behind enemy lines. He may not have invented anything but he is a pretty sharp mind and could easily read the odds. A victory was statistically impossible. Only Ehrendil was the wild card that tipped the balance in Elves' favour until now.

Adamar took matters into his own hands and built energy conduct and defensive structures right behind Ehrendil's front. More than once, he sent for reinforcement to Klaudel who was very evasive and slow to respond. If Ehrendil was a hero and a great inspiration to the troops, Adamar knew that the only way for the warriors to keep up this miracle was also to have walls and defensive structures to retreat to, until they charged back out again.

Adamar did the impossible and created a siege-like warfare to pressure the Orcs. His genius plan worked and intimidated the Orcs who never really saw clearly how many warriors they were fighting. The elves were fighting in a ratio of 1 to 15 in Adamar's estimation, and the odds were worsened every time an elf warrior fell.

He did come forward and confront his captain, Ehrendil. For all of his wisdom and loyal service, he received a slap to the face and was humiliated in front of what was left of the regiment. Adamar was furious and was going to leave. But he is not a deserter, imagine the shame on his father's name! Adamar loved dearly his father, Zeno.

But Adamar had no death wish either. Beyond the wall, there was the local population of Elves far from politics, sporadic pockets of old-ways elves here and there. If Klaudel is not sending reinforcement, recruiting the help of these locals was the only hope to stand until reinforcement arrives.

Captain Ehrendil heard about the rumour of dragons not far away. Ehrendil and a few of his warriors went on the quest for these dragons to capture and ride. Adamar took the opportunity to go quietly into the nearby forests to meet with locals. The defenses were holding, especially since the last days, the Orcs were not attacking anymore.

Facing such warriors as Ehrendil, they had changed their tactic to defensive, maybe looking for a way to pull him into a trap. That dragon story is surely a trap waiting to close on Ehrendil and his loyalists. Adamar was convinced of that.

Adamar's plan was simple, to hold the line until reinforcement comes and to disappear under the radar once the victory was secured. Warfare and politic are 2 of the things Adamar hated the most.

Adamar ran into the forest, looking for the Elves' habitat. He had a very short window before Ehrendil comes back or before the Orcs decide to push forward their attacks. Adamar needed to secure supplies to buy enough time until reinforcement arrives.

Running in the forest, Adamar was very careful to avoid any Orc patrol. They were pretty much everywhere. The first patrol he crossed path with missed him by a few trees. The second, he fooled them by crawling down in the thick grass. The third patrol, he heard them miles away. He simply avoids them. He was about to simply pass them by when he understood that they had a prisoner.

"That's none of your business Elf, move on. Many lives are depending on you! You are no hero. Keep your mission straight." That's what he was telling himself. But somehow, his body refused to listen and he approached. The prisoners were 2 Elf kids. They were 4 Orcs, no way Adamar could take all of them out, even with an energy blaster.

Adamar waited until 2 of the Orcs were close to a tree. He uses his blaster to throw half of the tree on them. Then, he jumped on the 3rd one and finished him up with the push of his blaster. Then, he felt someone smashing his head. Adamar was thrown to the ground. The 4th Orc approaches slowly with his ax ready to take a blow. One arrow stops the Orc right in between the eyes. Adamar turned around, there was a female elf warrior standing, with the bow in her arms. They freed the kids. Adamar was injured and passed out.

When he opened his eyes, he was in an Elf millennial tree under the care of his mysterious saviour. She thanked him, he saved her children. Adamar was still trying to make sense of what just happened. He thanked the lady but he had to return to his post, an Orc attack was imminent. He was in no condition to move.

The Elf lady's name was Loreleia Valvaris. She insisted for him to rest for the night. He won't survive the forest alone in the dark. By morning, he woke up and saw the lady putting up a fire, gathering the life force to cook their morning meal. That was so laborious. Adamar stood up, dressed up, and seized his energy blaster.

Within a few minutes, he drilled an energy pit and canalized the life force into useful energy. That was so easy since they were standing inside of a millennial tree. That made him into the hero, not only for the widow mom but for the entire village. They heard of such technology but had never before seen it in action. Loreleia was falling for the hero she rescued.

Adamar explained to everyone the reason for his presence and how he will need their help to defeat the Orcs. "The Orcs are destroying our habitat and killing our brothers and sisters. Whatever you need, we are Elves, we stand as one." That was mainly the response he received. They were ready to go to war with him. Adamar reassured them that he only needed them to provide supplies until reinforcement arrived.

"We would gladly but we barely have enough to feed our people. How could we supply your army too?" And once more, Adamar smiled. "All I need are your hands. I will upgrade each of your facilities with energy conduct, so you will be able to produce 10 times fold with the same work. That will more than suffice to supply the regiment."

Without losing a single more moment, he organized the workforce and the convoy to supply the army. He, himself, started foraging and installing energy conducts into each household, each facility.

Before the end of the night, food and supplies arrived at the fortification where the warriors celebrated the local help. For 3 days, Adamar upgraded the village into a supply outpost, enough to hold the siege for several more weeks. Now, he needed to convince Captain Klaudel to advance and secure the supply lines.

Adamar borrowed a wolf and mounted it to the fortified main outpost, the one that Klaudel's forces were holding. The ride was risky and very open but Adamar had to take the risk. Escorted by 2 Elf warriors, Adamar rid to find Klaudel. He found bored and hungry troops waiting for action.

Adamar explained the situation to the captain but Klaudel was firmed on following orders. Only the supply lines got him to listen to reason. Klaudel promised to advance his troop to secure the village and the supply lines. That was more than Adamar was hoping for.

At the front, Ehrendil and his Elves, came back victorious riding flying dragons. The legend was born again, the Knights were back! The abundance of supplies gave a boost of morale to the troops. The news of Klaudel advancing pushed Ehrendil to fast forward his own plans. He and his troops were the heroes, no way to let a coward come and share the glory. They will attack before the arrival of Klaudel.

That night, Ehrendil pressed the attack into the headquarter of the enemy with a few Dragon Knights and what was left from his regiment. He left the outpost with a handful of guards, just enough to greet Klaudel and his army. That's how arrogant Ehrendil was.

It was an almost empty, barely guarded outpost full of supplies that Adamar found on his return. He was mad! The foolish captain will get them all killed just to figure in songs! Very quickly, Adamar reorganized the supply lines and abandoned the outpost to secure the village. He took control of all the remaining soldiers and headed back to the village.

The only mission now was to keep the Orcs from discovering the supply lines and to wait for Klaudel's troops to stand their ground. Reinforcement from the 7 Metropolis was on its way. As soon as air support will be there, it would be over and the war will be won.

He went back to Loreleia and her children, and kept them safe, in the depth of the mines. They were hidden but they are still contributing to the war effort, using the energy blasters to forage and strengthen the supply lines.

In the front, Ehrendil made much damages, but he and his troops also endured the wrath of the Orcs, especially from Delmott who singly killed a third of the Elf forces and the dragons they were riding on. Ehrendil was forced to retreat with the few Knights still alive.

It was a close one, Delmott knew that he could not survive another assault like this one. It was a very shy victory, standing on such a thin line. It is then that Durz, arrived with intelligence from the field that Klaudel the other Elf captain is advancing with his troop. It seems that there was another mastermind to this war, his name was Adamar, not a warrior but an engineer.

She informed Delmott and went on to take care of that inconvenience. Delmott also received the report from his second in command, Smogulg. The entire herd was advancing, evacuating their colony. The lava had already burned most of their homes.

Delmott had no choice, he directed all of his soldiers to claim the East Outpost, the closest and where Ehrendil was stationed with his Knights. Tonight, they will feast inside of the Mildor's Gate or all hope will be lost.

Delmott took the lead and directed the offensive. More than 5000 orcs warriors were raining down on Mildor's Gate. Ehrendil and his Knights were nowhere to be found. The Orc easily wiped out the guards and took control of the fortifications.

They were settling in when Klaudel's troops arrived. Immediately, the Elves pressed the attack. Klaudel is no gambler but he will never see an Orc inside of Elf's fortification. By chance, Edrendil and his Knights arrived slightly after and joined in the combat. The violence lasted for the whole night.

By morning Delmott was still fighting but very few of his Orcs were left standing. This was History repeating itself. Delmott gave his life for the hope of salvation of his people. He held his ax close to his chest and met the enemy in combat until there was no life force left in him.

***

The news of the victory travelled in the forest and reached the village. The Elves rejoiced. Adamar was not convinced that the war was over, not until air support arrived. Adamar made sure that Loreleia and her kids were safe underground, in the mines. Since his return, Loreleia and him grew very close and he assured her that once reinforcement comes, they will leave for a peaceful life together.

In the meantime, he still has a war to win. He was pushing the mining and supply operation. In the middle of the night, he looked up and saw the lights of the air vessels lighting the dark sky. Mission accomplished.

Adamar did not have the time to even say a word, he felt his heart stop. He looked down and saw the blade through his chest. He felt a strong female presence pressed against him. That was not the presence of Loreleia, his promised love.

This is **The Book of Elves**, the second volume of **Prologues of Destiny**, the first trilogy.

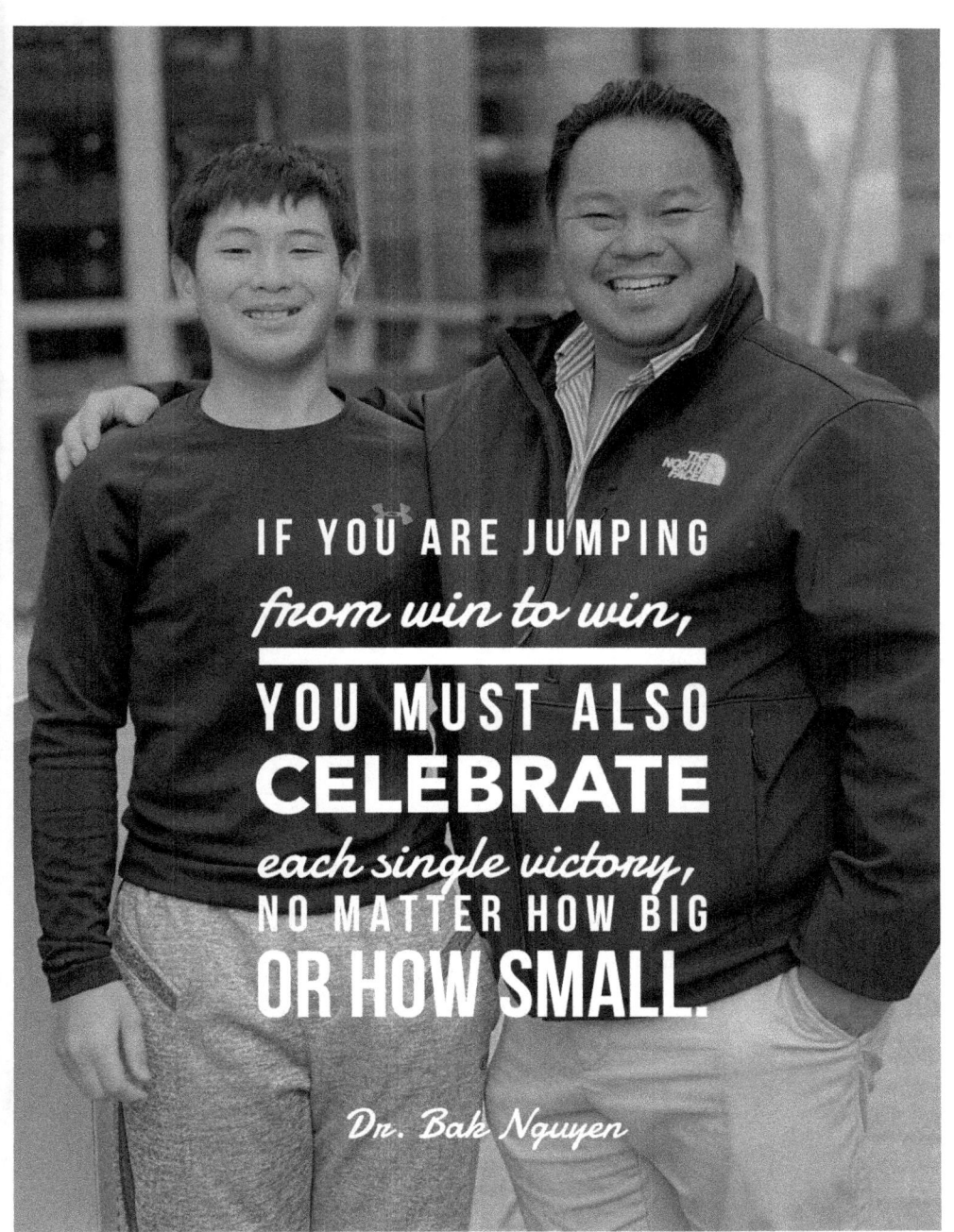

CHAPTER 15
"WE PLAYED THE STORY"
by William Bak

Honestly, when we started writing **THE BOOK OF ELVES**, I was off. I never really understood what it would be about and I did not care much. That was more my dad's book. We haven't even finished **PAPALAND** yet.

To be fair, that was trailing behind for the last few months. I guess, my father did not want to repeat what happened last year as we were stalling, and since **PAPALAND** was going nowhere after my grandpa torpedoed it, moving forward was the right thing to do.

For the first chapter, I did not really do much. My father wrote that one. My motivation was at ground level. To be honest, things went by so fast that I don't even remember when we wrote this book, but I can assure you, I did!

What I really remember were the celebrations in New York City. Wait, these were about the completion of **PAPALAND**. I wrote so much and so many books that I am a little confused.

What I can tell you is that **THE BOOK OF ELVES** is about the other planet in our universe, **DESTINY**, and about its inhabitants, the elves. The elves are fighting the orcs and like in any great action story, there are big battles!

As the book began, it was about the elves and their way of life. That was boring to me. But as soon as the war took place, I was all in. Who lives and who dies, we got heroes rising, some I never heard about before but as the story unfolded, I began to care. And care much I did.

To make it interesting, me and my dad were playing the video game, STARCRAFT 2 as a team against the computer. I just love that strategy game. Well, some of our games became the legendary battles in our book.

For the first book, we were playing Mobile Legends, a game on mobile. STARCRAFT 2 is a whole other level, playing on the computer with a mouse and everything. I still remember when I found the dick of the game and remember how much I dreamt about playing that game when I was younger.

We installed the game and spent so many evenings, not as father and son, but as teammates in a huge war. What is very special about this game is that we can watch the replay of our game after the facts. It is much like these sports teams reviewing their gameplay in between the matches.

I had much fun playing and strategizing with my dad. Oh, he was not always the one giving orders, the goal was to win. At first, I was learning how to play. Then we won. Then, I became cocky and we lost. My dad hates losing, so I was brought back in line.

> **"TO WIN, YOU NEED BOTH MONEY AND MINDSET. IF YOU HAVE THE MONEY AND NO MINDSET, YOU DON'T KNOW WHAT TO DO AND YOU LOSE. IF YOU HAVE THE MINDSET AND NO MONEY, IT IS USELESS."**
> WILLIAM BAK

When I said that to my parents in the car, that evening as we were driving back home, they both were so proud of me. I wasn't sure why they were so proud, I was just talking about the game.

I learnt a lot playing STARCRAFT 2. I learnt how important it is to have a good start. Then, I learnt how important it is to be a team player. I learnt to follow orders and eventually, I learnt to give orders. I was getting better game after game because we reviewed our games and my father was commenting on what I could improve. He was also kind enough (not just being an Asian dad) to recognize when I was doing good!

STARCRAFT 2 really bonded us. I was addicted and so was my dad. Some of the games lasted for more than 30 minutes and the battles were epic. Well, it was when we watched the replays that the battle scenes in **THE BOOK OF ELVES** came to life.

It is something to write about a battle and soldiers and swords. It is something else when you have actually felt their anger, fear, and frustration. Playing the game, you played as a general, ordering people around. Watching the replays, we got to follow these people and see how they went, survived, or died. That was really what made it so organic. We never decided who lives or dies, we just wrote about the games we played.

That was so fun. And since we played every evenings, writing **THE BOOK OF ELVES** went by so fast. I wrote my 500 words chapters, then, I was eager to go back to our "command center" to know what will arrive next.

In between the battles, writing to fill the storyline was made easy since we had 500+ characters already made to choose from. I guess, when I said that I don't remember writing that book, is because writing **THE BOOK OF ELVES** did not traumatize me! It was so much fun.

Before I knew it, we were in New York shooting videos about the release of our new book. The last time that we did that for **LEGENDS OF DESTINY**, was last fall, in Toronto. These trips have become a way for me to keep track of my life and my books as an author.

> "THE MOST FUN WE HAD WAS BECAUSE WE DID NOT WRITE THE STORY, WE PLAYED THE STORY."
> WILLIAM BAK

And like they say, the show must go on. We played, we celebrated and we moved on. Or should I say, we went back to **PAPALAND** to reboot that book. But that is another story. On **THE BOOK OF ELVES**, I think that people will love it. It really made the **LEGENDS OF DESTINY** real and organic.

This is the first volume of **THE RISE OF LEGENDS, to the moon and beyond**!

Welcome to the Alphas.

I will show you.
I won't force you.
But I won't wait for you.
Dr. Bak Nguyen
& William Bak

CHAPTER 16
"WE PLAYED THE STORY"
by Dr. Bak Nguyen

What did we do this time, you surely wonder? Well, after the completion and publication of the 2nd volume of **LEGENDS OF DESTINY, THE BOOK OF ELVES**, we were on fire. Right after publishing the manuscript to Amazon, I was working on the cover of the next volume to close the first trilogy of the series.

The 3rd volume will be titled **THE AGE OF DEMONS**. It was so easy to write about these universes and so fun to play with the 500+ characters that we have created. But wait, we had another book in the pipeline: **PAPALAND**!

We were stuck at 50%, with 4 chapters finished over 8 in total. I was not ready to let that one sink completely. I hacked the energy and momentum of **LEGENDS OF DESTINY** to push for the reboot and completion of **PAPALAND**.

William was not very happy about that idea but he too wasn't ready to throw away 50% of a book done. It took that and more transformers to convince him to come back to the writing-table. Within the next few weeks, we finished the script of **PAPALAND** on a high note!

A month ago, I was borderline depressed and empty, then the sun of the Dominican Republic put some sense back in me. About 30 days later, we were back on track and finished what we left behind. To celebrate the wins, we went to New York to shoot the next episode of my series **COVIDCONOMICS** and the launch of **THE BOOK OF ELVES**.

But New York was the stage for an even greater victory, the completion of **PAPALAND**! I can see how confusing that must be for you. Allow me to explain..

Referred to as a **LAUNCH** is once the book is available on Apple Books, Amazon COMBO paperback/audiobook, and Kindle. Once it is available internationally, we can set a book launch.

But since we stacked so many books one on top of the other and needed to celebrate every single win to keep our motivation, a **COMPLETION** of a book is once all the chapters are in. Sometimes, that even means that the correction process has not even begun yet.

Then, if and when the audiobook is accepted by AUDIBLE, which is the biggest global market for audiobooks, that is another win. We do not have a specific name for that process since not all of our books make it that far. By the time of this writing, a total of 5 of my books are distributed by AUDIBLE, 2 of mine, 2 co-written with William and William's first solo book.

And the ultimate level of our line of production is, so far, the **UAX** albums. At that stage, we reworked each chapter into soundtracks, with music and sound effects, just like in a Hollywood blockbuster movie. Those are pretty heavy in labor, time, and resources.

Once produced, they have to pass the selection of Apple Music, Spotify, Amazon Prime, and the other major outlets. This is a whole other process. Only a few selected titles make it this far. By the time of this writing, I have 7 **UAX** albums streaming.

Especially for the last category, with the **UAX** albums, I am in a league of my own. The streaming outlets do not have a category for Audiobooks with special effects. It took a while for them to start accepting our albums. Now you understand the work and the victory behind each of the words.

> "I COUNT WORLD RECORDS TO KEEP TRACK OF MY BOOKS BUT IF YOU MUST KNOW, THAT IS SIMPLY THE BEGINNING OF MY WORK."
> DR. BAK NGUYEN

So, we went to New York to celebrate our next win! That would be an understatement. I convinced Tranie to go to New York, a few weeks after we were back from Samana, in the Dominican Republic.

What I forgot to mention is that we opened our first expansion last month, a brand new dental clinic. That one was not easy. So many times, we were sure that the banks would pull the plug on us because of COVID. Well, after nearly 4 years in the pipeline, we finally inaugurated, very discreetly, the comeback of Mdex. That was mostly Tranie's victory.

That's the real reason why we were celebrating in New York. I leveraged that victory to set a dateline for William and myself to finish **PAPALAND** and it worked (that and more transformers)!

Actually, if I stop and count, **PAPALAND** is by far, the most expansive book in terms of Transformers! Nonetheless, we did it and finished with a huge win! Actually, the final ended up on such a great note that we went out celebrating in a big way, Frank Sinatra's way, in the Big Apple.

That was the inspiration I used to theme William's videos as he shared the ups and downs of writing **PAPALAND** in New York. The interviews went on LinkedIn and created such a wave of interest, a few weeks after his hit with the launch of **PAPA, J'SUIS PAS CON**. William's fan base was building up, not just silently, more and more people were now reaching out!

As father and son, we were on a high. After New York, we went to Quebec City, a few weeks later to celebrate the LAUNCH of **PAPALAND**. On the way there, we joked about what would happen next…

Have you guessed? The jokes started the laughing. Many laughs later, those laughs pushed the joke to the next level. Within the 2 and a half hours of drive between Montreal and Quebec City, we created **PAPALAND 2**.

It was funny, it was edgy, we simply had to do it. But motivation and inspiration were kind of very scarce. William and I both were very aware of the thin ice we were walking on. So what do you think that we shoot in Quebec City? We shot the **ANNOUNCEMENT** of our next project, **PAPALAND 2**.

Announcements are Hollywood products in which you give interviews about the upcoming projects to create hype and excitement. That is mostly a marketing and public relations effort.

Well, to us, it was our way to leverage our growing fan base to keep us accountable for what we set our minds on. Since we are both men of our words, now that the news is out, we had no other choice but to make it happen. And we did.

It took us 6 weeks to finish **PAPALAND 2**. That one was really, really hard. Not because we were lacking motivation, but because we raised the bar in script writing skills while we did not have a game to leverage on (as we have with **LEGENDS OF DESTINY**).

PAPALAND 2 is a book for kids, our Christmas tales books. No one dies in our Christmas tales, there can be ghosts, but no dead. That took away our secret weapon as scriptwriters. In **LEGEND OF DESTINY**, we have 500+ characters to play with, in comparison, **PAPALAND** has less than 20 characters.

To make the story work, I even had to borrow a ghost from a new coming-up series of mine, **PARADOX**. That gave up the fix we desperately needed.

If in **PAPALAND 1**, William, Hush, and myself were the main characters, in the 2nd volume of **PAPALAND**, only William and Hush would return. That was what made it so interesting at the beginning, as we kept building on William's frustration.

If at the beginning of **PAPALAND 1**, we were looking for the Recipe of the Perfect Father, in **PAPALAND 2**, it is simply about William's quest to go home! He has Hush as a loyal companion, and some, not even all of the 5 original PAPAS back, and some new ones.

If you must know, it really felt like what Hollywood screenwriters are going through to write a sequel to a big hit, trying to keep it original and interesting.

Of course, **PAPALAND 2** cost me more Transformers. I set up a dateline too, mid-May 2022 as it would coincide with our trip to Florida to attempt conventions and business meetings.

By now, you must know us.

We shot in Miami the **COMPLETION** of **PAPALAND 2**. William had submitted his final chapters. It was now upon my shoulders to review and embellish his chapters. That took me the following weeks.

By June 2022, **PAPALAND 2** was released in ebook on Apple Books and Kindle, and on COMBO paperback/audiobook on Amazon. No Audible nor **UAX** yet. Those too will come, but I am running short in time, with my landmark world records dateline coming fast, by the end of August.

By the time of this writing, I am still 10 books short of setting the next landmark world record. I am so short on time and energy that I don't even know if I could make it to 120 books by the end of August. Sure, I won these kinds of challenges the last 2 years, but this year, I am running low and I am feeling much older.

With the completion of this book, I would be 9 books away from 120 books. And that is to add that I am already banking on the extra 4 I wrote last year to push from 96 to 100 to make it look better!

And surely **PAPALAND** 1 and 2 did not help with my landmark world records but they marked the beginning of a new era for me as a writer.

Don't even bother asking, there is no **PAPALAND 3** on the table. But we also said after the first one that there won't be a second one... I guess, only time will tell.

This is the first volume of **THE RISE OF LEGENDS, to the moon and beyond**!

Welcome to the Alphas.

> I will show you.
> I won't force you.
> But I won't wait for you.
> Dr. Bak Nguyen
> & William Bak

ACHIEVER OF THE YEAR LINKEDIN AWARD AND TOWN HALL
NOMINEE EY ENTREPRENEUR OF THE YEAR
LYS GRAND HOMAGE DIVERSITY

WILLIAM BAK **DR. BAK NGUYEN**

AU PAYS DES PAPAS 2
MAIS ON S'EN FOUT!

WORLD TOP100 DOCTOR

CHAPTER 17
"PAPALAND 2"
by William Bak & Dr. Bak Nguyen

You have no idea with how much pride and joy, William and I are proud to present to you **PAPALAND 2**. There were surely much road bumps and distractions on the way. Especially as we said that **PAPALAND 1** was final.

To not spoil the story of neither **PAPALAND** 1 or 2, I decided to share with you the first chapter of **PAPALAND 2**. Beware, it is catchy and you might end up buying that book to read the rest of the story! This is the translation of the first chapter of PAPALAND 2, from its French original edition, **AU PAYS DES PAPAS 2**. Enjoy!

EPISODE 1
"THE AWAKENING"
by William Bak & Dr. Bak Nguyen

William wakes up. However, he feels so tired, just as if he had just come out of a long adventure or a dream that never ends.

He is alone in a huge king bed. Strange, he doesn't remember having such a big bed.

He looks around and his room is so clean that he could barely recognize it. All the toys are in their place, every single one of them. There are even very rare Transformers models that he does not remember having received but dreamt of, looking over the internet. Something is really strange. This is too good to be true!

On one side, there are Transformers, collector's items that would make the greatest collectors salivate and on the other, he sees a Lego city with several electric trains crossing the city. Decidedly, he is still dreaming, of a very beautiful dream!

-Master William, breakfast is served! Starts a very kind feminine voice.

A beautiful, slender mature woman enters the room with a tray. William caught a cold and had a fever all night. He must now regain his strength. William recognizes this beautiful familiar presence, but he cannot remember her name. He digs into his memories so much that his head hurts. Finally, he notices that the lady has a name tag, her name is Edith.

Of course, Edith! How could he forget her name? But Edith is William's governess in the first Christmas story!!! She is not real! William is not sure what is happening to him, he must be still dreaming! None of this makes sense, but he holds back to remain calm and in control.

Edith sets the silver tray on the bed and gently touches William's forehead to make sure that the fever is indeed gone. William is lost in his thoughts. Luckily, Edith did not see that, she just assumed that William was still asleep. If she would suspect that something is wrong, William would be in bed for the rest of the week. Definitely, there is no more fever.

- Master William, today you stay in bed. I've prepared a nice hot soup that should give you back on your feet and at full strength!
- Soup? But I hate soup!
- You haven't even tasted it yet, it's a recipe from my grandmother! She makes the best mushroom soup!
- Mushrooms!!!! No, no, no, no...

William is seizing in panic at that last word, mushroom! That, he has not forgotten! Stomach ache, farts, grenades, papas, and spiders! He must wake up, now! Normally, he would have slapped himself, but he remembers that it doesn't work here. And even in a dream, the slap really hurts!

Edith looks at a very troubled master William, not understanding what was really going on. She sees the drops of sweat appearing on his forehead. Worried, she touches William's forehead again. He's soaked, but he doesn't have any fever.

- Master William, eat a little and you'll feel better, I promise you.
- No, please, I hate soups and mushrooms, they make me sick!
- Just a taste, for me.

Edith smiled tenderly at him. She is so nice and William doesn't want to hurt her feelings. He closes his eyes and opens his mouth hesitantly.

- Wow, that's really good!
- I told you! That's my grandmother's secret recipe. Now open your mouths again, aah!

Edith does not need to repeat herself, William takes the spoon from her hands and tackles the soup. Funny breakfast in bed but it is a real treat! His stomach does not hurt, on the contrary, he feels so much better. This dream is a different dream and the mushrooms do not have the same powers.

After devouring the soup, William gets up to go to the bathroom. There's just one small problem, he doesn't know where the bathroom is. Scratching his head, he asks Edith where is the toilet?

- Are you still that sleepy, Master William? There are 21 toilets in the mansion, the nearest toilet is just to your right. Are you sure that you are alright?

William gets up, very embarrassed. He knows that Edith suspects that something is wrong. He marches quickly into the bathroom to avoid further questioning from Edith. He knows her, if she thinks that something's wrong, she will put him to bed for days!

William cannot take that risk. He disappears into the toilet. He looks in the mirror and recognizes himself. At least some things haven't changed. Thank God!

Edith surprises him again, holding a toothbrush with toothpaste in her hand, waiting for William. William does not understand, it's kind of weird. She tells him to open his mouth. Very shy, William obeys. Edith starts brushing his teeth!

No, this cannot be! He saw that in the movies of princes and princesses. In this dream, is he a prince? Who knows, it would be really great to be Royalty after the last dream in Papaland.

- Edith, am I a prince?
- Of course, you are, you are my own little prince, Master William. As for the others, you have to ask them. Mr. Paul, William asks if he is a prince?

The butler, Paul was just passing by. Paul is a man in his early sixties, robust, very square, with hunter's eyes. He can be very intimidating, especially to a child.

- Madame?
- Mr. Paul, William wants to know if he is a prince?
- Prince or not, he got the royal treatment this morning with breakfast in bed and personalized grooming. I'm sure that even Kings aren't treated so well!
- Don't be jealous Mr. Paul, if you're nice, I'll make some soup too!

William, who was following the conversation with his eyes, saw Mr. Paul blush before disappearing. He was embarrassed. And William too, he's not used to being so spoiled! His father would never have allowed anyone to brush his teeth!

Embarrassed, William takes his toothbrush from Edith's hands and finishes himself. Edith is proud of her little prince.

- Edith, where are my parents?
- They were supposed to be back yesterday, but a snowstorm grounded their plane in Canada!
- In Canada?! But where are we?
- What do you mean by where are we?
- What city are we in?
- But New York, of course. Are you sure that you are feeling well, Master William?

William knows that once again, he has talked too much. He must divert Edith's attention. He quickly changes the subject.

- I can't wait to see my parents.
- I know, they always come back with so many nice gifts for you! Especially since it is Christmas in a few days.
- Edith, can I have more mushroom soup, please?

With these words, William sees Edith's face blooming from her smile. She is such a beautiful lady. She reassures William that there is a big bowl waiting for him downstairs and that he must hurry before Mr. Paul finds it!

That was close! He dodged Edith's doubts and further questioning. She went down to the kitchen to warm up the soup. William was afraid that she would ground him in bed for the rest of the day. Where is his father? He must find Dr. Bak and find a way out of this dream!

But before he can get out of this dream, he must first find his way in this huge mansion! There are endless hallways and there are so many doors. Where is the kitchen?

- **I can help you?**

William raises his head and recognizes Mr. Paul who does not look very happy.

- **No, I was just looking for a new way to get to the kitchen. You know that is a fun game find new paths to get to the same point. You should come with me, Edith is waiting for us with her magical and delicious soup!**

Hearing Edith's name, the face of Mr. Paul changes. He's suddenly less serious, almost younger. At the thought of soup, he smiles, but not for very long. William noticed all of that. He knows he is still in a dream and Mr. Paul strangely reminds him of someone he knows: Solo!

After 2 big bowls of soup, William needs to stretch. He goes out to the backyard of the mansion. There is a park overlooking the water. Only once he has met all of Edith's requirements in terms of clothing, William finally receives the authorization to go out in the park. Edith could be very strict.

Outside, it is snowing. It was truly magical. All of the trees are white, and decorated with lights. Is it the charm of winter or rather the magic of Christmas? William closes his eyes and looks up to feel the snowflakes falling and melting on his face.

It's such a feeling of freedom and of well-being. This is such a different dream from the last one at Papaland, Grumpy, Doncare, Drooling, and Solo. Hush would have liked to run in this huge park, she would have hunted all the spiders by herself...

In the midst of his reverie, the inevitable happens: William feels the effects of the mushrooms, once again.

His gases, involuntarily released, quickly dissipate the vastness of the park and of Winter. No one was even around to notice. This was without any consequences. But then, William is suddenly pulled from his reverie by a snowball in his face!

- Got you!

Very Surprised, William turns around but there is no one. Who threw that snowball? William is all alone in this huge park. That was easy to know since there were only his footsteps in the snow. But where are the other children?

He explores the wide paths of the park, and he will find the person who threw the snowball at him. William hears a distant laugh. He turns around and boom! Once more, he eats a snowball right in the face. This time, he had his mouth open and the snow got to the back of his throat!

- That's disgusting! Wait, I'm going to make you eat some snow! Show yourself, you coward!

William shakes off the snow quickly and he arms himself with snowballs, one in each hand. He turns and looks everywhere, he is still the only soul in that park! He continues to circle the trees. Finally, he sees a shadow in the wood. He approaches with very light steps. This time, it's his turn to have fun!

He approaches and, as soon as he is within reach, he throws with everything that he got, the 2 snowballs. Right on target! William threw the snowballs and hit them right in the face, twice! He just doesn't know who ate them. It is time to know who threw him these snowballs. It is a very unhappy Mr. Paul whom he sees wiping himself off and recovering from his surprise!

- **Who did that? Yells a Mr. Paul, ax in hand.**

William hid. Fortunately, he is much faster than Mr. Paul who has not seen him. To be honest, Mr. Paul scares William. He doesn't seem very friendly, he doesn't have Edith's tenderness and he can be very intimidating.

William catwalks towards the house to escape Mr. Paul's wrath. He crosses the park unseen. Just before entering the back door, he hears the same mocking laugh, again. He turns around and eats a third snowball in the face. This time, the blow is so violent that he falls.

William gets up quickly. This time, it's too much, he's angry!

- **Who did that?**

Was it Paul who took his revenge? He turns around and sees Mr. Paul opening the door of the house behind him.

- Did they get you too? Mr. Paul asks with a very, very serious tone.
- Who did that?
- Probably the kids in the neighbourhood. I thought that the kids of rich people were well educated! Come in Master William, before they get to you again.

William didn't know what to think. Was Mr. Paul having fun with him or was there someone else in the park? Whatever, but William very distinctly heard a drooling laugh... No, that's not possible. This is impossible, can that be Drooling? But that's a whole other dream!

William was pulled from his reflection by another laugh, one that he would recognize from anywhere: a warm big laugh, kind and joyful. It's Grandpa! William runs toward Grandpa and throws himself into the arms of his favourite Grandpa!

They spent a long afternoon at the toy store, with bags full of goodies! Grandpa is so nice, with him, it is always fun! William ate more slices of cheese pizza than his belly could handle. He and Grandpa had a competition to see who would eat the most pizzas. Grandpa lost! They both pushed the challenge too far and both fell asleep in front of the fireplace laughing with a stomach ache!

It's finally Hush's barking that wakes William from his sleep. He feels very squeezed. As he remembered, there was so much room before, now, everything is so tight. Grandpa hugged him, but once the fire went out, he hugged him even tighter to keep him warm. William turns his head as he comes slowly back to life and he sees other arms hugging him too, many, many other arms. He wakes up sweating!v

To his surprise, he recognizes Solo, Doncare, Grumpy, and Drooling, all hugging him and his Grandpa. They were all asleep and snoring in symphony. Hush keeps barking happily, that's how she greets William!

- Hush, I've missed you so much, starts William! Don't you speak in this dream?

For answer, he only receives more barking with the symphony of snores as background. William knew it, I knew that he recognized the mocking laughter of Drooling earlier. He silently approaches Drooling and gently pulls him towards the living room table where a glass of cold water was at the edge.

William has prepared his move with attention. At 3, he shouts TIMBER in the ears of Drooling who wakes up, hits the table, and drops the cold water right on his face!

- Good morning, shouts out William, very satisfied with his retaliation on Drooling.

Everyone would have thought that Drooling's scream would wake up all the other papas, but no, it was Edith's screams that pulled everyone from their dreams and back on their feet!

From the kitchen, Edith was screaming at the top of her lungs. Everyone rushed to her aid.

This is **PAPALAND 2.** Welcome to the Alphas.

THERE ARE NO PERFECT FATHERS.
WHAT'S IMPORTANT IS THAT THEY ARE THERE
FOR THEIR KIDS.

Dr. BAK NGUYEN

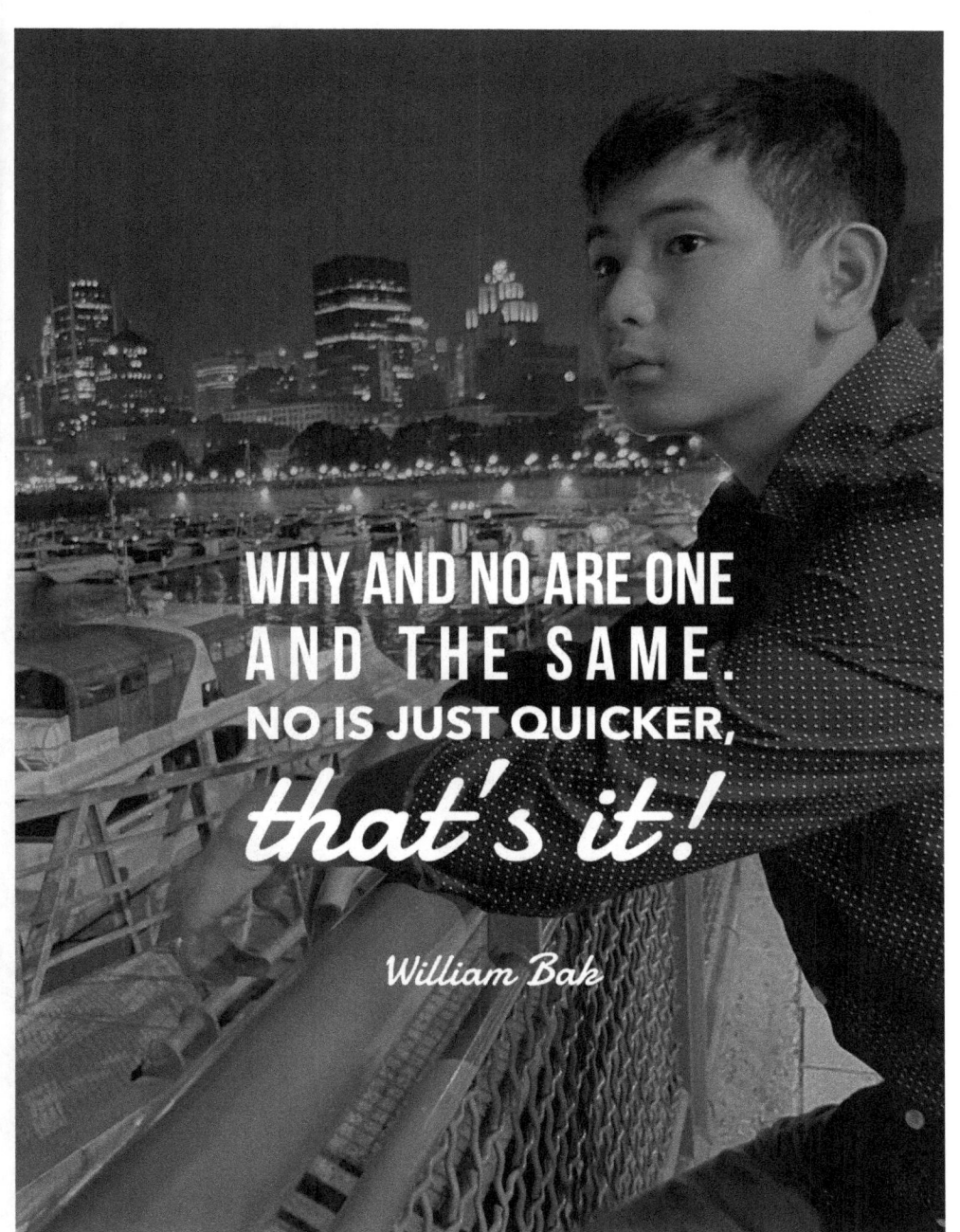

CHAPTER 18
"THIS IS NOT THE END"
by William Bak

Let's go back to the first book of **PAPALAND**. When we finally finished that one, by the second take, the conclusion was so great that it got us ideas, crazy and silly ideas. Yep, the idea of reviving the writing a second book came on the table.

I laughed and put an abrupt NO to that. My father agreed too, finishing the first **PAPALAND** was of the domain of the impossible. I still couldn't believe that we found ways to save that one from sinking. And believe me, now it is such a great story!

But then, the joke kept coming in, on how I would wake up, in a different dream and still not home yet. And my dad would be nowhere to be found, in that dream! We made so many jokes the following days that my dad fooled me into saying yes, again.

That cost him some new transformers but we moved forward. Believe it or not, I was happy to do so. But I also know that we have to move very quickly before we lose our motivation.

> "WRITING BOOKS, I LEARNT HOW IMPORTANT MOTIVATION IS.
> IT MAKES THE DIFFERENCE BETWEEN PAIN AND FUN."
> WILLIAM BAK

That was how **PAPALAND 2** came to the table. But my dad had another reason to write a second book. When we wrote the first book, they were 2 beginning of stories to introduce us as characters. Well, as we rebooted the storyline, you know, after the torpedoes, these stories never got to make sense. But since the beginning of the book was perfect, we decided to leave them as is.

Now that we had the chance to keep telling the story in **PAPALAND 2**, my father wanted to go back to close the loop on those. He started by making me (my character) awake in the bed of the rich master William in his mansion, with his governess and his butler. Hush and grandpa were both in that storyline too. The only person missing was my dad. That was perfect!

Writing the reboot of **PAPALAND, THE BOOK OF LEGENDS** and now, **PAPALAND 2**, I learnt much about the rules of storytelling, and the difference between writing for a book, a TV series, or a movie.

I learnt about how to make and evolve characters, I learnt about answering the questions in the story of each of the characters. No one can simply be there, everyone serves a purpose, sooner or later.

If I said in the first **PAPALAND** that we will be writing episodes instead of chapters, in **PAPALAND 2**, the choice became crystal clear. This one was about writing the script for a movie feature.

At first, that did not make much difference to me but as we were moving forward, I could see how hard it was to always put our heroes in trouble and to get them out to just end up in even more trouble!

I will say it again, writing **PAPALAND 2** was one of the most difficult experiences that I had, writing books. Not for the same reasons as writing **PAPALAND 1** which was the lack of motivation. The difficulties I faced writing **PAPALAND 2** were finding more and more ways to keep the story interesting and keep saving my heroes from impossible situations.

Actually, me, I wrote, it is my dad who had to fix most of the storyline. If in New York, we celebrated the completion of **PAPALAND**, in Quebec City, we celebrated its release. We also took that opportunity to announce that we would be starting **PAPALAND 2.**

We said that on camera to make sure that we would not back out from that one. Then, we wrote. The following weeks were simply crazy. Then, my parents had to travel for business to

Miami. That served as our dateline to have something to announce.

3 weeks after Quebec, I was in Miami, on video, announcing the completion of **PAPALAND 2**. That was true for me, my dad still had to work on the last 2 chapters. For these two, I went all in with 700 and 800 words per chapter respectively.

On a Miami rooftop, that was simply crazy! I was so proud of myself and could not believe how far we went. But that was it, I now have to prepare for the exams ahead coming from the Ministry of Education. That was serious stuff since I have to finish elementary school and go on to high school next year.

There are so many actions and jokes packed in **PAPALAND 2**, you have no idea. If we lost motivation writing **PAPALAND 1**, motivation was flowing freely, coming from all the jokes we invented from **PAPALAND 2**.

It may be very hard to write but I like it so much, and you will too, I am sure of that! What was also funny was watching my dad struggle to finish the book. He had to work with my 700 and 800 words chapters and make sense of everything. I think that it took him a whole week to finish the last chapter of that book. One whole week! We are talking about Dr. Bak, the world record author who wrote 100 books in 4 years!

That was surely very entertaining to watch, especially when I was done! You have no idea of the satisfaction that I had, to be ahead of my dad!

This year writing started big with my solo book and ended in an even greater note, of me being ahead of my dad! I have improved much on my writing skills, and my vocabulary, in both, French and English.

There are no more free books where all I have to do was to talk. That last year, I wrote 500 words chapters to earn my name on the cover of each of them. What we are writing is more and more interesting, so much that I can see **LEGENDS OF DESTINY** and **PAPALAND** on TV eventually.

I am far from done, now that it is fun, I am just getting started. After the **RISE OF LEGENDS**, **THE AGE OF DEMON**, the 3rd volume of **LEGENDS OF DESTINY** is next, and I can't wait to start that one!

This is the first volume of **THE RISE OF LEGENDS, to the moon and beyond**!

Welcome to the Alphas.

> I will show you.
> I won't force you.
> But I won't wait for you.
> Dr. Bak Nguyen
> & William Bak

CONCLUSION

by Dr. Bak Nguyen

Wow, this year was a hell of a ride with William. Actually, it has been our busiest year of writing together, ever. Sure, there were years when we wrote more books, but those were children's books with about 5000 words on average. Now, each of our books are ranging between 15,000 and 25,000 words.

Our books have reached my standards as a prolific writer, both in pace and volume. If you add the production of video interviews, Audiobooks, and **UAX** albums, the partnership between William and myself, has produced the most advanced products and results of my career as an author.

"WILLIAM IS MY SECRET WEAPON."
DR. BAK NGUYEN

After 4 years of writing together, actually, we started writing together by December 2018; so after 43 months of writing as co-authors, as father and son, we have:

- the trilogies of the Legend of the Chicken Heart x2

- 1 dragon book (**WE ARE ALL DRAGONS**) x2
- 7 chicken books x2
- 2 Legends of Destiny
- 2 PAPALAND books
- 1 Vaccin books (And 1 translated in Spanish) x2
- 1 Mastermind book (**TIME MANAGEMENT ON STEROIDS**)
- 1 trilogy of parenting (**THE BOOKS OF LEGENDS**)

And this one, **THE RISE OF LEGENDS**, the first volume of a new trilogy. And the x2 are because we wrote them twice, to release them in English and in French. That's a total of 33 books in 43 months. Add to that his solo book, **PAPA, J'SUIS PAS CON** and he has signed 34 books within 43 months.

For a kid of 12-year-old, that indeed sets him in a league of his own, with many world records and landmark world records. I can't express enough how proud I am of my son, William Bak, the little boy who wanted to write books with his father, as he was 7.

It came to the point that everyone could see a brotherhood between the 2 of us. As William is growing, I am becoming more and more a big brother than a father. I always said that I couldn't care less about the labels. We play games together, we challenge one another and we are partners in my coming back to Hollywood.

That gave me the chance to grow by his side and him, by mine. Today, we are more brothers than father and son. That is no understatement, we watch SUPERNATURAL and we are seeing ourselves within the relationship of the Winchester brothers.

Then, we watch FRIENDS, the classic sitcom, and it is too obvious to say that William and I share the same kind of relationship Chandler and Joey are sharing. And that's not just us, Tranie is saying that too! This is the first time that I share with you such details.

Well, I must admit that William changed me as much as I changed him. Well, I am the dad, it is my job to educate him. But for the last 4 years, I took my own medicine, opening up my heart and mind to grow side by side with my kid, and we wrote History together.

> "WE MADE HISTORY AS FATHER AND SON, WRITING MORE AND MORE STORIES."
> DR. BAK NGUYEN

This last year was a great one. Well, until the time of this writing, I did not realize how intense and concentrated on William, was my 5th year as a writer. Sure, I had my **ALPHA DENTISTRY** and **COVIDCONOMICS** series, but by far, my focus was on William and our magical connection.

> "I WILL SHOW YOU. I WON'T FORCE YOU, BUT I WON'T WAIT FOR YOU."
> DR. BAK NGUYEN & WILLIAM BAK

That is what I taught my son. That is also what I did for close to 2 years, pushing and getting my mark to the landmark world record of 100 books written in 4 years. I was proud but as I looked back at William, I was afraid of a self-prophetized conclusion.

I was so relieved when he wrote his first solo book to celebrate my 100th and to beat me at my own game. Then, together, we started new paths and new adventures, writing fiction together. On the way, we had ups and downs, fun and less but we always had each other.

If for the first 3 years, William was more talking and I was writing, this last year, he wrote 500 words per chapter, minimum, to join our books. He is writing in English and in French, which doesn't make any difference to either one of us anymore. Sure, there are misspellings here and there, but one chapter after the next, he is getting better and better, in French, in English, but especially using words and storytelling skills.

The mistake I made was to ask William to write once with a pencil and a notebook, a real one. That killed the magic. Since then, I gave him his own laptop and he is writing on his own, managing his own schedule.

We meet to agree on what book to write and the important plots of the story. We create the characters, and we draft the plan for the 8 chapters of our books. And more and more, William is taking the lead. Once he submits his chapter, I basically rewrite each of them, often respecting his plot points but adding more details, jokes, dialogues, and intrigues.

Once I finish writing the final chapter, I send it for recording. Chapters are taking a life of their own once we sit together to listen to the audiobook. If we are blown away by our own script, the idea of bringing music and sound effects will be next on the table, with the **UAX** protocols. That's pretty much our process.

If the **UAX** albums are not exclusive to William's books with me, they are the most prominent to be upgraded as such. Now that William has even started writing solo books, I have high hope for him.

What I still do on my own are the covers, the editing and publishing of our chapters into books, and all of the graphics surrounding the characters, and sometimes, the video editing of our trailers, interviews, and **PRETRAILERS**.

What is a **PRETRAILER** you might ask? Well, I created those as we were working on **LEGENDS OF DESTINY**, to edit a Hollywood-style movie trailer to launch a new storyline or a new character. I know, it sounds crazy since everyone in the movie industry will write a script first and have a movie made later.

The trailer is the last step since it is edited from the footage of the movie. But with the advancement of technology and the abundance of royalty-free libraries online, I am embracing those to kickstart our projects.

I made 2 **PRETRAILERS** for **LEGENDS OF DESTINY** and they propelled our inspiration to the next level. For our next franchise, **PARADOX**, I already made 3 **PRETRAILERS**. Actually, one of those saved me in the writing of **PAPALAND** 2 when I hit a wall in the storyline.

If last year, I was not as prolific in terms of the number of books, I was in research and development mode and delivered big time for our debut writing fiction.

That meant a lot to me personally since I wrote novels and stories 30 years ago and never published any of them. Then, I elevated myself to have a shot at Hollywood, but that too, I let go, embracing my dental licence and my title as a doctor instead.

Writing fiction is heavy in emotions, ghosts, and regrets for me. William guided me through my comeback. Holding his hand and laughing with him, I defeated my demons, got back to the dark woods, found my powers, and rose!

I often express to William how much I love him. I do not hide my emotions of gratitude of having him as a son and a partner. But, I guess, I never took the time to give him the real weight of recognition of what he has done for me, helping me to face my regrets and to come back to move forward! From the bottom of my heart, William, thank you!

Your love brought back the magic that I forgot.
Your love released powers I held inside and forgot.
Your presence is kind and exciting,
That, I will never forget.

This could have been **THE BOOK OF LEGENDS 4**, instead, I decided to start a new trilogy with **THE RISE OF LEGENDS**. Rise, because it is really what this is, our rise, my comeback, and our great adventures as co-writers, as father and son, as brothers.

What's coming next? Well, the 3rd book of **LEGENDS OF DESTINY, THE AGE OF DEMONS** is burning to be written. Then, William agreed to join my next franchise too, **PARADOX**, which is a story that I created 25 years ago. William also has a few solo books planned on his own. No worries, I will be there to support him.

Moving forward, we will leverage the power of the **PRETRAILERS** more and more, the power of gaming to write more franchises, and to produce more **UAX** Albums. Actually, our books together will be leveraging my invention to stream stories and entertain the world. It is my intention to make the **UAX** Albums production into the flagship of my books with William.

Yes, we are dreaming. Yes, we are aiming for the moon. And yes, we are having much fun doing so. For the last 4 years, we broke the **sound barrier** together. I don't know about you, but to me, the moon will simply be a stop. What's beyond?

Yes, this is serious. Now that I had 30 months in COVID to reflect on my life and my choices, I am coming back to the dream that I left behind, some 21 years ago.

I have announced to my partners and patients that I would retire more or less within the next 3 years from active dentistry. I have these 3 years to transition into my life purpose, of what I love to do and can do without over-stretching myself: telling stories.

Writing books is my genius and with the **UAX** lines, that is as close as I can be to Hollywood and movie-making on my own. But wait, I am not alone. I have a whole team and even more people believing in me. I have fans and I have the means to make things happen.

What was really missing was the will to come back to writing fiction. Well, William took care of that hesitation of mine, of what was holding me back.

I am not alone, I am a wingman, a young man who grew up by my side and who is challenging me to always push to the next level, for more and more while having fun!

"NO FUN, NO GAME."
WILLIAM BAK

I am moving forward knowing that I am not leaving anything behind. If for now years, I've learnt that I can't get too attached to anything or anyone, it was still hard to apply that philosophy completely, especially when you are a father. Well, William made that easy for me, walking by my side.

Stick around and you will be seeing more and more of us. Now that we have found each other, there is so much more magic coming your way!

This is the first volume of **THE RISE OF LEGENDS, to the moon and beyond**!

Welcome to the Alphas.

I will show you.
I won't force you.
But I won't wait for you.
Dr. Bak Nguyen
& William Bak

ANNEX
GLOSSARY OF Dr. BAK's LIBRARY

1

1SELF -080

REINVENT YOURSELF FROM ANY CRISIS
BY Dr. BAK NGUYEN

In 1SELF is about to reinvent yourself to rise from any crisis. Written in the midst of the COVID war, now more than ever, we need hope and the know-how to bridge the future. More than just the journey of Dr. Bak, this time, Dr. Bak is sharing his journey with mentors and people who built part of the world as we know it. Interviewed in this book, CHRISTIAN TRUDEAU, former CEO and FOUNDER of BCE EMERGIS (BELL CANADA), he also digitalized the Montreal Stock Exchange. RON KLEIN, American Innovator, inventor of the magnetic stripe of the credit card, of MLS (Multi-listing services) and the man who digitalized WALL STREET bonds markets. ANDRE CHATELAIN, former first vice-president of the MOVEMENT DESJARDINS. Dr. JEAN DE SERRES, former CEO of HEMA QUEBEC. These men created billions in values and have changed our lives, even without us knowing. They all come together to share their experiences and knowledge to empower each and everyone to emerge stronger from this crisis, from any crisis.

AFTERMATH -063
BUSINESS AFTER THE GREAT PAUSE
BY Dr. BAK NGUYEN & Dr. ERIC LACOSTE

In AFTERMATH, Dr. Bak joins forces with Community leader and philanthrope Dr. Eric Lacoste. Two powerful minds and forces of nature in the reaction to the worst economic meltdown in modern times. We are all victims of the CORONA virus. Both just like humans have learned to adapt to survive, so is our economy. Most business structures and management philosophies are inherited from the age of industrialization and beyond. COVID-19 has shot down the world economy with months. At the time of the AFTERMATH, the truth is many corporations and organizations will either have to upgrade to the INFORMATION AGE or disappear. More than the INFORMATION upgrade, the era of SOCIAL MEDIA and the MILLENNIALS are driving a revolution in the core philosophy of all organizations. Profit is not king anymore, support is. In this time and age where a teenager with a social account can compete with the million dollars PR firm, social implication is now the new cornerstone. Those who will adapt will prevail and prosper, while the resistance and old guards will soon be forgotten as fossils of a past era.

ALPHA DENTISTRY vol. 1 -104
DIGITAL ORTHODONTIC FAQ
BY Dr. BAK NGUYEN

In ALPHA DENTISTRY, DIGITAL ORTHODONTICS FAQ, Dr. Bak is looking to democratize the science of dentistry, starting with orthodontic. In a word, he is sharing everything a patient needs to know on the matter in FAQ form. In order to make the knowledge complete and universal, Dr. Bak has invited Alpha Dentists from all around the world to join in and to answer the same question. With Alpha Dentist from America and Europe, ALPHA DENTISTRY is the first effort to create a universal knowledge in the field of dentistry, starting with orthodontics. ALPHA DENTISTRY, DIGITAL ORTHODONTICS FAQ is in response to the COVID crisis, the shortage of staff crisis, and the effort to unify dentistry to the Information Age, as discussed in RELEVANCY and COVIDCONOMICS, THE DENTAL INDUSTRY.

ALPHA DENTISTRY vol. 1 -109
DIGITAL ORTHODONTIC FAQ ASSEMBLED EDITION
USA SPAIN GERMANY INDIA CANADA
BY Dr. BAK NGUYEN, Dr. PAUL OUELLETTE, Dr. PAUL DOMINIQUE, Dr. MARIA KUNSTADTER, Dr. EDWARD J. ZUCKERBERG, Dr. MASHA KHAGHANI, Dr. SUJATA BASAWARAJ, Dr. ALVA AURORA, Dr. JUDITH BÄUMLER, and Dr. ASHISH GUPTA

In ALPHA DENTISTRY, DIGITAL ORTHODONTICS FAQ, Dr. Bak is democratizing the science of dentistry, starting with orthodontics. In a word, he is sharing everything a patient needs to know on the matter in FAQ form, simple words you'll understand.10 International Alpha Doctors, from USA, Spain, Germany, India, and Canada are joining forces to make the knowledge complete and universal. ALPHA DENTISTRY is the first effort to create a universal knowledge in the field of dentistry, this is the orthodontics volume. This is the most ambitious book project in the History of Dentistry. ALPHA DENTISTRY is in response to the COVID crisis, the shortage of staff crisis, and the effort to unify dentistry to the Information Age, as discussed in RELEVANCY and COVIDCONOMICS, THE DENTAL INDUSTRY.

ALPHA DENTISTRY vol. 1 -113
DIGITAL ORTHODONTIC FAQ INTERNATIONAL EDITION
ENGLISH SPANISH GERMAN HINDI FRANÇAIS
BY Dr. BAK NGUYEN, Dr. PAUL OUELLETTE, Dr. PAUL DOMINIQUE, Dr. MARIA KUNSTADTER, Dr. EDWARD J. ZUCKERBERG, Dr. MASHA KHAGHANI, Dr. SUJATA BASAWARAJ, Dr. ALVA AURORA, Dr. JUDITH BÄUMLER, and Dr. ASHISH GUPTA

In ALPHA DENTISTRY, DIGITAL ORTHODONTICS FAQ, Dr. Bak is democratizing the science of dentistry, starting with orthodontics. In a word, he is sharing everything a patient needs to know on the matter in FAQ form, simple words you'll understand.10 International Alpha Doctors, from USA, Spain, Germany, India, and Canada are joining forces to make the knowledge complete and universal. ALPHA DENTISTRY is the first effort to create a universal knowledge in the field of dentistry, this is the orthodontics volume. This is the most ambitious book project in the History of Dentistry. ALPHA DENTISTRY is in response to the COVID crisis, the shortage of staff crisis, and the effort to unify dentistry to the Information Age, as discussed in RELEVANCY and COVIDCONOMICS, THE DENTAL INDUSTRY.

ALPHA LADDERS -075
CAPTAIN OF YOUR DESTINY
BY Dr. BAK NGUYEN & JONAS DIOP

In ALPHA LADDERS, Dr. Bak is sharing his private conversation and board meetings with 2 of his trusted lieutenants, strategist Jonas Diop and international Counsellor, Brenda Garcia. As both the Dr. Bak and ALPHA brands are gaining in popularity and traction, it was time to get the movement to the next level. Now, it's about building a community and to help everyone willing to become ALPHAS to find their powers. Dr. Bak is a natural recruiter of ALPHAS and peers. He also spent the last 20 years plus, training and mentoring proteges. Now comes the time to empower more and more proteges to become ALPHAS. ALPHAS LADDERS is the journey of how Dr. Bak went from a product of Conformity to rise into a force of Nature, know as a kind tornado. In ALPHA LADDERS Jonas pushed Dr. Bak to retrace each of the steps of his awakening, steps that we can breakdown and reproduce for ourselves. The goal is to empower each willing individual to become the ultimate Captain of his or her destiny, and to do it, again and again. Welcome to the Alphas.

ALPHA LADDERS 2 -081
SHAPING LEADERS AND ACHIEVERS
BY Dr. BAK NGUYEN & BRENDA GARCIA

In ALPHA LADDERS 2, Dr. Bak is sharing the second part of his private conversation and board meetings with his trusted lieutenants. This time it is with international Counsellor, Brenda Garcia that the dialogue is taking place. In this second tome, the journey is taken to the next level. If the first tome was about the WHYs and the HOWs at an individual level, this tome is about the WHYs and the HOWs at the societal level. Through the lens of her background in international relations and diplomacy, Brenda now has the mission to help Dr. Bak establish structures, not only for his emerging organization and legacy, THE ALPHAS, but to also inspire all the other leaders and structures of our society. To do this, Brenda is taking Dr. Bak on an anthropological, sociological and philosophical journey to revisit different historical key moments in various fields and eras, going as far back as in ancient Greece at the dawn of democracy, all the way to the golden era of modern multilateralism embodied by the UN structure. Learning from the legacies of prominent figures going from Plato to Ban Ki Moon, Martin Luther King or Nelson Mandela, to Machiavelli, Marx and Simone de Beauvoir, Brenda and Dr. Bak are attempting to grasp the essence of structure and hierarchy, their goal being to empower each willing individual to become the ultimate Captain of their own success, to climb up the ladders no matter how high it is, and to build their legacy one step at a time.

AMONGST THE ALPHAS -058
BY Dr. BAK NGUYEN, with Dr. MARIA KUNDSTATER, Dr. PAUL OUELLETTE and Dr. JEREMY KRELL

In AMONGST THE ALPHAS Dr. Bak opens the blueprint of the next level with the hope that everyone can be better, bigger, wiser, but above all, a philosophy of Life that if, well applied, can bring inspiration to life. The Alphas rose in the midst of the COVID war as an International Collaboration to empower individuals to rise from the global crisis. Joining Dr. Bak are some of the world thinkers and achievers, the Alphas. Doctors, business people, thinkers, achievers, influencers, they are coming together to define what is an Alpha and his or her role, making the world a better place. This isn't the American dream, it is the human dream, one that can help you make History.Joining Dr. Bak are 3 Alpha authors, Dr. Maria Kundstater, Dr. Paul Ouellette and Dr. Jeremy Krell. This book started with questions from coach Jonas Diop. Welcome to the Alphas.

AMONGST THE ALPHAS vol.2 -059
ON THE OTHER SIDE
BY Dr. BAK NGUYEN with Dr. JULIO REYNAFARJE, Dr. LINA DUSEVICIUTE and Dr. DUC-MINH LAM-DO

In AMONGST THE ALPHAS 2, Dr. Bak continues to explore the meaning of what it is to be an Alpha and how to act amongst Alphas, because as the saying taught us: alone one goes fast, together we goes far. Some people see the problem. Some people look at the problem, some people created the problem. Some people leverage the problem into solutions and opportunities. Well, all of those people are Alphas. Networking and leveraging one another, their powers and reach are beyond measure. And one will keep the other in line too. Joining Dr. Bak are 3 Alphas from around the world coming together to share and collaborate, Dr. DUSEVICIUTE, Dr. LAM-DO and Dr. REYNAFARJE. This isn't the American dream, it is the human dream, one that can help you make History. Welcome to the Alphas.

AU PAYS DES PAPAS -106
BY Dr. BAK NGUYEN & WILLIAM BAK

On ne nait pas papa. On le devient. Dans sa quête d'être le meilleur papa possible pour William, Dr. Bak monte au pays des papas avec William à la recherche du papa parfait. Comme pour tout dans la vie, il doit exister une recette pour faire des papas parfaits. AU PAYS DES PAPAS est le récit des souvenirs des papas que Dr. Bak a croisé avant, alors et après qu'il soit devenu papa lui aussi. Une histoire drôle et innocente pour un Noël magique, ceci est la nouvelle aventure de William et de son papa, le Dr. Bak. Entre les livres de poulet, LEGENDS OF DESTINY et les des livres parentaux de Dr. Bak, AU PAYS DES PAPAS nous amène dans le monde magique de ces êtres magiques qui forgent des rêves, des vies et des destins.

AU PAYS DES PAPAS 2 -108
BY Dr. BAK NGUYEN & WILLIAM BAK

On ne nait pas papa, ça on le sait après le premier voyage AU PAYS DES PAPAS. Suite à leur première expédition, Dr. Bak et William ont compris qu'il n'y a pas de papas parfaits ni de recette pour faire des papas parfaits. Pourtant, les papas parfaits existent! Dans ce 2e récit AU PAYS DES PAPAS, William revient avec son papa, Dr. Bak, mais cette fois, c'est William qui dirige l'expédition. Même s'il n'existe pas de recette pour faire des papas parfaits, il doit toutefois exister des façons de rendre son papa meilleur, version 2.0! C'est la nouvelle quête de William et du Dr. Bak, à la recherche de la mise-à-jour parfaite pour le meilleur papa 2.0 possible! William est déterminé à tout pour trouver la recette cette fois-ci! AU PAYS DES PAPAS 2 est le nouveau récit des aventures père-fils du Dr. Bak et de William Bak, après AU PAYS DES PAPAS 1, les livres de poulets, LEGENDS OF DESTINY et les BOOKS OF LEGENDS.

B

BOOTCAMP -071
BOOKS TO REWRITE MINDSETS INTO WINNING STATES OF MIND
BY Dr. BAK NGUYEN

In BOOTCAMP 8 BOOKS TO REWRITE MINDSETS INTO WINNING STATES OF MIND, Dr. Bak is taking you into his past, before the visionary entrepreneur, before the world records, before the Industry's disruptor status. Here are 8 of the books that changed Dr. Bak's thinking and, therefore, reset his evolution into the course we now know him for. BOOTCAMP: 8 BOOKS TO REWRITE MINDSETS INTO WINNING STATES OF MIND, is a Bootcamp of 8 weeks for anyone looking to experience Dr. Bak's training to become THE Dr. BAK you came to know and love. This book will summarize how each title changed Dr. Bak mindset into a state of mind and how he applied that to rewrite his destiny. 8 books to read, that's 8 weeks of Bootcamp to access the power of your MIND and of your WILL. Are you ready for a change?

BRANDING -044
BALANCING STRATEGY AND EMOTIONS
BY Dr. BAK NGUYEN

BRANDING is communication to its most powerful state. Branding is not just about communicating anymore but about making a promise, about establishing a relation, about generating an emotion. More than once, Dr. Bak proved himself to be a master, communicating and branding his ideas into flags attracting interest and influences, nationally and internationally. In BRANDING, Dr. Bak shares a very unique and personal journey, branding Dr. Bak. How does he go from Dr. Nguyen, a loved and respected dentist to becoming Dr. Bak, a world anchor hosting THE ALPHAS in the medical and financial world?More than a personal journey, BRANDING helps to break down the steps to elevate someone with nothing else but the force of his or her spirit. Welcome to the Alphas.

CHANGING THE WORLD FROM A DENTAL CHAIR -007
BY Dr. BAK NGUYEN

Since he has received the EY's nomination for entrepreneur of the year for his startup Mdex & Co, Dr. Bak Nguyen has pushed the opportunity to the next level. Speaker, author, and businessman, Dr. Bak is a true entrepreneur and industries' disruptor. To compensate for the startup's status of Mdex & Co, he challenged himself to write a book based on the EY's questionnaire to share an in-depth vision of his company. With "Changing the World from a dental chair" Dr. Bak is sharing his thought process and philosophy to his approach to the industry. Not looking to revolutionize but rather to empower, he became, despite himself, an industries disruptor: an entrepreneur who has established a new benchmark. Dr. Bak Nguyen is a cosmetic dentist and visionary businessman who won the GRAND HOMAGE prize of "LYS de la Diversité" 2016, for his contribution as a citizen and entrepreneur in the community. He also holds recognitions from the Canadian Parliament and the Canadian Senate.

In 2003, he founded Mdex, a dental company upon which in 2018, he launched the most ambitious private endeavour to reform the dental industry, Canada wide. He wrote seven books covering ENTREPRENEURSHIP, LEADERSHIP, QUEST of IDENTITY, and now, PROFESSION HEALTH. Philosopher, he has close to his heart the quest of happiness of the people surrounding him, patients, and colleagues alike. Those projects have allowed Dr. Nguyen to attract interests from the international and diplomatic community and he is now the centre of a global discussion on the wellbeing and the future of the health profession. It is in that matter that he shares with you his thoughts and encourages the health community to share their own stories.

CHAMPION MINDSET -039
LEARNING TO WIN
BY Dr. BAK NGUYEN & CHRISTOPHE MULUMBA

CHAMPION MINDSET is the encounter of the business world and the professional sports world. Industries' Disruptor Dr. BAK NGUYEN shares his wisdom and views with the HAMMER, CFL Football Star, Edmonton's Eskimos CHRISTOPHE MULUMBA on how to leverage on the champion mindset to create successful entrepreneurs. Writing and challenging each other, they discovered the parallels and the difference of both worlds, but mainly, the recipe for leveraging from one to succeed in the other, from champions and entrepreneurs to WINNERS. Build and score your millions, it is a matter of mindset! This is CHAMPION MINDSET.

EMPOWERMENT -069
BY Dr. BAK NGUYEN

In EMPOWERMENT, Dr. Bak's 69th book, writing a book every 8 days for 8 weeks in a row to write the next world record of writing 72 books/36 months, Dr. Bak is taking a rest, sharing his inner feelings, inspiration, and motivation. Much more than his dairy, EMPOWERMENT is the key to walk in his footsteps and to comprehend the process of an overachiever. Dr. Bak's helped and inspired countless people to find their voice, to live their dream, and to be the better version of themselves. Why is he sharing as much and keep sharing? Why is he going that fast, always further and further, why and how is he keeping his inspiration and momentum? Those are all the answers EMPOWERMENT will deliver to you. This book might be one of the fastest Dr. Bak has written, not because of time constraints but from inspiration, pure inspiration to share and to grow. There is always a dark side to each power, two faces to a coin. Well, this is the less prominent facets of Dr. Bak Momentum and success, the road to his MINDSET.

F

FORCES OF NATURE -015
FORGING THE CHARACTER OF WINNERS
BY Dr. BAK NGUYEN

In FORCES OF NATURE, Dr. Bak is giving his all. This is his 15 books written within 15 months. It is the end of a marathon to set the next world record. For the occasion, he wanted to end with a big bang! How about a book with all of his biggest challenges? A Quest of Identity, a journey looking for his name and powers, Dr. Bak is borrowing with myths and legends to make this journey universal. Yes, this is Dr. Bak's mythology. Demons, heroes and Gods, there are forces of Nature that we all meet on our way for our name. Some will scare us, some will fight us, some will manipulate us. We can flee, we can hide, we can fight. What we do will define our next encounter and the one after. A tale of personal growth, a journey to find power and purpose, Dr. Bak is showing us the path to freedom, the Path of Life. Welcome to the Alphas.

HORIZON, BUILDING UP THE VISION -045
VOLUME ONE
BY Dr. BAK NGUYEN

Dr. Bak is opening up at your demand! Many of you are following Dr. Bak online and are asking to know more about his lifestyle. This is how he has chosen to respond: sharing his lifestyle as he traveled the world and what he learned in each city to come to build his Mindset as a driver and a winner. Here are 10 destinations (over 69 that will be following in the next volumes...) in which he shares his journey. New York, Quebec, Paris, Punta Cana, Monaco, Los Angeles, Nice, Holguin, the journey happened over twenty years.

HORIZON, ON THE FOOTSTEP OF TITANS -048
VOLUME TWO
BY Dr. BAK NGUYEN

Dr. Bak is opening up at your demand! Many of you are following Dr. Bak online and are asking to know more about his lifestyle. This is how he has chosen to respond: sharing his lifestyle as he traveled the world and what he learned in each city to come to build his Mindset as a driver and a winner. Here are 9 destinations (over 72 that will be following in the next volumes...) in which he shares his journey. Hong Kong, London, Rome, San Francisco, Anaheim, and more…, the journey happened over twenty years. Dr. Bak is sharing with you his feelings, impressions, and how they shaped his state of mind and character into Dr. Bak. From a dreamer to a driver and a builder, the journey started since he was 3. Wealth is a state of mind, and a state of mind is the basis of the drive. Find out about the mind of an Industry's disruptor.

HORIZON, DREAMING OF THE FUTURE -068
VOLUME THREE
BY Dr. BAK NGUYEN

Dr. Bak is back. From the midst of confinement, he remembers and writes about what life was, when traveling was a natural part of Life. It will come back. Now more than ever, we need to open both our hearts and minds to fight fear and intolerance. Writing from a time of crisis, he is sharing the magic and psychological effect of seeing the world and how it has shaped his mindset. Here are 9 other destinations (over 75) in which he shares his journey. Beijing, Key West, Madrid, Amsterdam, Marrakech and more…, the journey happened over twenty years.

HOW TO TO BOOST YOUR CREATIVITY TO NEW HEIGHTS -088
BY Dr. BAK NGUYEN

In HOW TO BOOST YOUR CREATIVITY TO NEW HEIGHTS, Dr. Bak is sharing his secrets of creativity and insane production pace with the world. Up to lately, Dr. Bak shared his secrets about speed and momentum but never has he opened up about where he gets his inspiration, time and time again. To celebrate his new world record of writing 100 books in 4 years, Dr. Bak is joined by his proteges strategist Jonas Diop, international counsellor Brenda Garcia and prodigy William Bak for the writing of his secrets on creativity. Brenda, Jonas and William all have witnessed Dr. Bak creativity. This time, they will stand in to ask the right questions to unleash that creative power in ways for others for follow the trail. Part of the MILLION DOLLAR MINDET series, HOW TO BOOST YOUR CREATIVITY TO NEW HEIGHTS is Dr. Bak's open book to one of his superpower.

HOW TO NOT FAIL AS A DENTIST -047
BY Dr. BAK NGUYEN

In HOW TO NOT FAIL AS A DENTIST, Dr. Bak is given 20 plus years of experience and knowledge of what it is to be a dentist on the ground. PROFESSIONAL INTELLIGENCE, FINANCIAL INTELLIGENCE and MANAGEMENT INTELLIGENCE are the fields that any dentist will have to master for a chance to success and a shot for happiness practicing dentistry. Where ever you are starting your career as a new graduate or a veteran in the field looking to reach the next level, this is book smart and street smart all into one. This is Million Dollar Mindset applied to dentistry. We won't be making a millionaire out of you from this book, we will be giving you a shot to happiness and success. The million will follow soon enough.

HOW TO WRITE A BOOK IN 30 DAYS -042
BY Dr. BAK NGUYEN

In HOW TO WRITE YOUR BOOK IN 30 DAYS, Dr. Bak has crafted writing skills and techniques that can be shared and mastered. This book is mainly about structure and how to keep moving forward, avoiding the hit of the INSPIRATION WALL. You will find a wealth of wisdom from his experience writing your first, second, or even 10th book. Dr. Bak is sharing his secrets writing books, having written himself 72 books within 36 months. Visionary businessman, doctor in dentistry, Dr. Bak describes himself as a Dentist by circumstances, a communicator by passion, and an entrepreneur by nature.

HOW TO WRITE A SUCCESSFUL BUSINESS PLAN -049
BY Dr. BAK NGUYEN & ROUBA SAKR

In HOW TO WRITE A SUCCESSFUL BUSINESS PLAN, Dr. Bak is given 20 plus years of experience and knowledge of what it is to be an entrepreneur and more importantly, how to have the investors and banks on your side. Being an entrepreneur is surely not something you learn from school, but there are steps to master so you can communicate your views and vision. That's the only way you will have financing.Writing a business is only not a mandatory stop only for the bankers, but an essential step to every entrepreneur, to know the direction and what's coming next. A business plan is also not set in stone, if there is a truth in business is that nothing will go as planned. Writing down your business plan the first time will prepare you to adapt and to overcome the challenges and surprises. For most entrepreneurs, a business is a passion. To most investors and all banks, a business is a system. Your business plan is the map to that system. However unique your ideas and business are, the mapping follows the same steps and pattern.

HUMILITY FOR SUCCESS -051
BALANCING STRATEGY AND EMOTIONS
BY Dr. BAK NGUYEN

HUMILITY FOR SUCCESS is exploring the emotional discomforts and challenges champions, and overachievers put themselves through. Success is never done overnight and on the way, just like the pain and the struggles aren't enough, we are dealing with the doubts, the haters, and those who like to tell us how to live our lives and what to do. At the same time, nothing of worth can be achieved alone. Every legend has a cast of characters, allies, mentors, companions, rivals, and foes. So one needs the key to social behaviour. HUMILITY FOR SUCCESS is exploring the matter and will help you sort out beliefs from values, peers from friends. Humility is much more about how we see ourselves than how others see us. For any entrepreneur and champion, our daily is to set our mindset right, and to perfect our skills, not to fit in. There is a world where CONFIDENCE grows is in synergy with HUMILITY. As you set the right label on the right belief, you will be able to grow and to leave the lies and haters far behinds. This is HUMILITY FOR SUCCESS.

HYBRID -011
THE MODERN QUEST OF IDENTITY
BY Dr. BAK NGUYEN

I

IDENTITY -004
THE ANTHOLOGY OF QUESTS
BY Dr. BAK NGUYEN

What if John Lennon was still alive and running for president today? What kind of campaign will he be running? IDENTIFY -THE ANTHOLOGY OF QUESTS is about the quest each of us has to undertake, sooner or later, THE QUEST OF IDENTITY. Citizen of the world, aim to be one, the one, one whole, one unity, made of many. That's the anthology of life! Start with your one, find your unity, and your legend will start. We are all small-minded people anyway! We need each other to be one! We need each other to be happy, so we, so you, so I, can be happy. This is the chorus of life. This is our song! Citizens of the world, I salute you! This is the first tome of the IDENTITY QUEST. FORCES OF NATURE (tome 2) will be following in SUMMER 2021. Also under development, Tome 3 - THE CONQUEROR WITHIN will start production soon.

INDUSTRIES DISRUPTORS -006
BY Dr. BAK NGUYEN

INDUSTRIES DISRUPTORS is a strange title, one that sparkles mixed feelings. A disruptor is someone making a difference, and since we, in general, do not like change, the label is mostly negative. But a disruptor is mostly someone who sees the same problem and challenge from another angle. The disruptor will tackle that angle and come up with something new from something existent. That's evolution! In INDUSTRIES DISRUPTORS, Dr. Bak is joining forces with James Stephan-Usypchuk to share with us what is going on in the minds and shoes of those entrepreneurs disrupting the old habits. Dr. Bak is changing the world from a dental chair, disrupting the dental, and now the book industry. James is a maverick in the Intelligence space, from marketing to Artificial Intelligence. Coming from very different backgrounds and industries, they end up telling very similar stories. If disruptors change the world, well, their story proves that disruptors can be made and forged. Here's the recipe. Here are their stories.

K

KRYPTO -040
TO SAVE THE WORLD
BY Dr. BAK NGUYEN & ILYAS BAKOUCH

L

L'ART DE TRANSFORMER DE LA SOUPE EN MAGIE -103
PAR Dr. BAK NGUYEN

Dans L'ART DE TRANSFORMER DE LA SOUPE EN MAGIE, Dr. Bak remonte aux sources pour connaître la source de son génie et la recette qui a été transféré à son fils, William Bak, auteur et record mondial dès l'âge de 8 ans. Docteur en médecine dentaire, entrepreneur, écrivain record mondial, musicien, Dr. Bak est d'abord et avant tout un fils qui a une maman qui croit en lui. L'ART DE TRANSFORMER DE LA SOUPE EN MAGIE est dédié à la recette du génie, celle qui pousse une mère a mijoté les ingrédients de l'espoir dans un bouillon d'amour, à y ajuster un zeste de bonheur et un brin d'ambition. Dans la lignée des livres parentaux de Dr. Bak, L'ART DE TRANSFORMER DE LA SOUPE EN MAGIE est dédié à la première femme dans sa vie, celle qui a tracé son destin et celle qui l'a cultivée.

LEADERSHIP -003
PANDORA'S BOX
BY Dr. BAK NGUYEN

LEADERSHIP, PANDORA'S BOX is 21 presidential speeches for a better tomorrow for all of us. It aims to drive HOPE and motivation into each and every one of us. Together we can make the difference, we hold such power. Covering themes from LOYALTY to GENEROSITY, from FREEDOM and INTELLIGENCE to DOUBTS and DEATH, this is not the typical presidential or motivational speeches that we are used to. LEADERSHIP PANDORA'S BOX will surf your emotions first, only to dive with you to touch the core and soul of our meaning: to matter. This is not a Quest of Identity, but the cry to rally as a species, to raise our heads toward the future, and to move forward as a WHOLE. Not a typical Dr. Bak's book, LEADERSHIP, PANDORA'S BOX is a must-read for all of you looking for hope and purpose, all of us, citizens of the world.

LEVERAGE -014
COMMUNICATION INTO SUCCESS
BY Dr. BAK NGUYEN

In LEVERAGE COMMUNICATION TO SUCCESS, Dr. Bak shares his secret and mindsets to elevate an idea into a vision and a vision into an endeavour. Some endeavours will be a project, some others will become companies, and some will grow into a movement. It does not matter, each started with great communication.Communication is a very vast concept, education, sale, sharing, empowering, coaching, preaching, entertaining. Those are all different kinds of communication. The intent differs, the audiences vary, the messages are unique but the frame can be templated and mastered. In LEVERAGE COMMUNICATION TO SUCCESS, Dr. Bak is loyal to his core, sharing only what he knows best, what he has done himself. This book is dedicated to communicating successfully in business.

LEGENDS OF DESTINY vol.1 -101
THE PROLOGUES OF DESTINY
BY Dr. BAK NGUYEN & WILLIAM BAK

The war between the forces of death and the legions of life lasted for centuries, ravaging most of the twin planets, Destiny and Earth. The end was so imminent that even the Gods got involved to save life from eternal doom.Heroes rise and fall from all sides. Some fight for good, others, for evil. Gods, titans, angels, demons all took sides in the war. Gods fight and kill other gods. Angel fights alongside demons, striking down Gods and Titans, and rival angels. The war lasted for so long that no one even remembers what they were fighting for. Some fight for domination while others, just to survive,. The war ravages Destiny, the twin sister of planet Earth to the brink of annihilation. All eyes now turn to Earth. As the balance of the creation itself hands in the balance, a species emerges as holding the balance to victory: mankind. For the future of Humanity, of Gods and men and everything in between, this is the last stand of Destiny, a last chance for life.

LEGENDS OF DESTINY vol.2 -107
THE BOOK OF ELVES
BY Dr. BAK NGUYEN & WILLIAM BAK

Caught between the Orcs invading from the center of Destiny, the Angels raining down and the Demons eating from within, the Elves are turning from their old beliefs and Gods for salvation. For Millennials, Elves turned to Odin and the Forces of Nature for answers and guidance. Since the imminent destruction of their kingdoms and cities, a new God is offering Hope, Kal, the old God of fire. Kal gave them more than Hope, he gave the elves who turned to him passage to a new world. But more than hope, more than fear, Elves value honour and Destiny. At least their old guards and heroes do. With their world crumbling down, the rise of the new and younger generations, Elf's society seem to be at the crossroad of evolution. It is convert or die. Or die fighting or die kneeling. The Book of Elves is the story of a civilization facing its fate at the blink of destruction.

MASTERMIND, 7 WAYS INTO THE BIG LEAGUE -052
BY Dr. BAK NGUYEN & JONAS DIOP

MASTERMIND, 7 WAYS INTO THE BIG LEAGUE is the result of the encounter of business coach Jonas Diop and Dr. Bak. As a professional podcaster and someone always seeking the truth and ways to leverage success and performance, coach Jonas is putting Dr. Bak to the test, one that should reveal his secret to overachieve month after month, accumulating a new world record every month. Follow those two great minds as they push each other to surpass themselves, each in their own way and own style. MASTERMIND, 7 WAYS INTO THE BIG LEAGUE is more than a roadmap to success, it is a journey and a live testimony as you are turning the pages, one by one.

MIDAS TOUCH -065
POST-COVID DENTISTRY
BY Dr. BAK NGUYEN, Dr. JULIO REYNAFARJE AND Dr. PAUL OUELLETTE

MIDAS TOUCH, is the memoir of what happened in the ALPHAS SUMMIT in the midst of the GREAT PAUSE as great minds throughout the world in the dental field are coming together. As the time of competition is obsolete, the new era of collaboration is blooming. This is the 3rd book of the ALPHAS, after AFTERMATH and RELEVANCY, all written in the midst of confinement. Dr. Julio Reynafarje is bearing this initiative, to share with you the secret of a successful and lasting relationship with your patients, balancing science and psychology, kindness, and professionalism. He personally invited the ALPHAS to join as co-author, Dr. Paul Ouellette, and Dr. Paul Dominique, and Dr. Bak.Together, they have more than 100 years of combined experience, wisdom, trade, skills, philosophy, and secrets to share with you to empower you in the rebuilding of the dental profession in the aftermath of COVID. RELEVANCY was about coming together and to rebuild the future. MIDAS TOUCH is about how to build, one treatment plan at a time, one story at a time, one smile at a time.

MINDSET ARMORY -050
BY Dr. BAK NGUYEN

MINDSET ARMORY is Dr. Bak's 49th book, days after he completed his world record of writing 48 books within 24 months, on top of being a CEO of Mdex & Co and a full-time cosmetic dentist. Dr. Bak is undoubtedly an OVERACHIEVER. From his last books, he has shared more and more of his lifestyle and how it forged his winning mindset. Within MINDSET ARMORY, Dr. Bak is sharing with us his tools, how he found them, forged them, and leverage them. Just like any warrior needs a shield, a sword, and a ride, here are Dr. Bak's. For any entrepreneur, the road to success is a long and winding journey. On the way, some will find allies and foes. Some allies will become foes, and some foes might become allies. In today's competitive world, the only constant is change. With the right tool, it is possible to achieve. The right tool, the right mindset. This is MINDSET ARMORY.

MIRROR -085
BY Dr. BAK NGUYEN

MIRROR is the theme for a personal book. Not only to Dr. Bak but to all of us looking to reach beyond who and what we actually are. MIRROR is special in the fact that it is not only the content of the book that is of worth but the process in which Dr. Bak shared his own evolution. To go beyond who we are, one must grow every day. And how do you compare your growth and how far have you reach? Looking in the mirror. In all of Dr. Bak's writing, looking at the past is a trap to avoid at all costs. Looking in the mirror, is that any better? Share Dr. Bak's way to push and keep pushing himself without friction nor resistance. Please read that again. To evolve without friction or resistance... that is the source of infinite growth and the unification of the Quest for Power and the Quest of Happiness.

MOMENTUM TRANSFER -009
BY Dr. BAK NGUYEN & Coach DINO MASSON

How to be successful in your business and in your life? Achieve Your Biggest Goals With MOMENTUM TRANSFER. START THE BUSINESS YOU WANT - AND BRING IT NEXT LEVEL! GET THE LIFE YOU ALWAYS WANTED - AND IMPROVE IT! TAKE ANY PROJECTS YOU HAVE - AND MAKE IT THE BEST! In this powerful book, you'll discover what a small business owner learned from a millionaire and successful entrepreneur. He applied his mentor's principles and is explaining them in full detail in this book. The small business owner wrote the book he has always wanted to read and went from the verge of bankruptcy to quadrupling his revenues in less than 9 months and improve his personal life by increasing his energy and bring back peacefulness. Together, the millionaire and the small business owner are sharing their most valuable business and life lessons to the world. The most powerful book to increase your momentum in your business and your life introduces simple and radical life-changing concepts: Multiply your business revenues by finding the Eye of your Momentum - Increase your energy by building and feeding your own Momentum - How to increase your confidence with these simple steps - How to transfer your new powerful energy into other aspects of your business and life - How to set goals and achieve them (even crush them!)- How to always tap into an effortless and limitless force within you- And much, much more!

P

PLAYBOOK INTRODUCTION -055
BY Dr. BAK NGUYEN

In PLAYBOOK INTRODUCTION, Dr. Bak is open the door to all the newcomers and aspirant entrepreneurs who are looking at where and when to start. Based on questions of two college students wanting to know how to start their entrepreneurial journey, Dr. Bak dives into his experiences to empower the next generation, not about what they should do, but how he, Dr. Bak, would have done it today. This is an important aspect to recognize in the business world, the world has changed since the INFORMATION AGE and the advent of the millenniums into the market. Most matrix and know-how have to be adapted to today's speed and accessibility to the information. We are living at the INFORMATION AGE, this book is the precursor to the ABUNDANCE AGE, at least to those open to embrace the opportunity.

PLAYBOOK INTRODUCTION 2 -056
BY Dr. BAK NGUYEN

In PLAYBOOK INTRODUCTION 2, Dr. Bak continuing the journey to welcome the newcomers and aspirant entrepreneurs looking at where and when to start. If the first volume covers the mindset, the second is covering much more in-depth the concept of debt and leverage. This is an important aspect to recognize in the business world, the world has changed since the INFORMATION AGE and the advent of the millenniums into the market. Most matrix and know-how have to be adapted to today's speed and accessibility to the information. We are living at the INFORMATION AGE, this book is the precursor to the ABUNDANCE AGE, at least to those open to embrace the opportunity.

POWER -043
EMOTIONAL INTELLIGENCE
BY Dr. BAK NGUYEN

IN POWER, EMOTIONAL INTELLIGENCE, Dr. Bak is sharing his experiences and secrets leveraging on his EMOTIONAL INTELLIGENCE, a power we all have within. From SYMPATHY, having others opening up to you, to ACTIVE LISTENING, saving you time and energy; from EMPATHY, allowing you to predict the future to INFLUENCE, enabling you to draft the future, not to forget the power of the crowd with MOMENTUM, you are now in possession of power in tune with nature, yourself. It is a unique take on the subject to empower you to find your powers and your destiny. Visionary businessman, doctor in dentistry, Dr. Bak describes himself as a Dentist by circumstances, a communicator by passion, and an entrepreneur by nature.

POWERPLAY -078
HOW TO BUILD THE PERFECT TEAM
BY Dr. BAK NGUYEN

In POWERPLAY, HOW TO BUILD THE PERFECT TEAM, Dr. Bak is sharing with you his experience, perspective, and mistake traveling the journey of the entrepreneur. A serial entrepreneur himself, he started venture only with a single partner as team to build companies with a director of human resources and a board of directors. POWERPLAY is not a story, it is the HOW TO build the perfect team, knowing that perfection is a lie. So how can one build a team that will empower his or her vision? How to recruit, how to train, how to retain? Those are all legitimate questions. And all of those won't matter if the first question isn't answered: what is the reason for the team? There is the old way to hire and the new way to recruit. Yes, Human Resources is all about mindset too! This journey is one of introspection, of leadership, and a cheat sheet to build, not only the perfect team but the team that will empower your legacy to the next level.

PROFESSION HEALTH - TOME ONE -005
THE UNCONVENTIONAL QUEST OF HAPPINESS
BY Dr. BAK NGUYEN, Dr. MIRJANA SINDOLIC, Dr. ROBERT DURAND AND COLLABORATORS

Why are health professionals burning out while they give the best of themselves to heal the world? Dr. Bak aims to break the curse of isolation that health professionals face and establish a conversation to start the healing process. PROFESSION HEALTH is the basis of an ongoing discussion and will also serve as an introduction to a study lead by Professor Robert Durand, DMD, MSc Science from University of Montreal, study co-financed by Mdex and the Federal Government of Canada. Co-writers are Dr. Mirjana Sindolic, Professor Robert Durand, Dr. Jean De Serres, MD and former President of Hema Quebec, Counsel-Minister Luis Maria Kalaff Sanchez, Dr. Miguel Angel Russo, MD, Banker Anthony Siggia, Banker Kyles Yves, and more… This is the first Tome of three, dedicated to help "WHITE COATS" to heal and to find their happiness.

R

REBOOT -012
MIDLIFE CRISIS
BY Dr. BAK NGUYEN

MidLife Crisis is a common theme to each of us as we reach the threshold. As a man, as a woman, why is it that half of the marriages end up in recall? If anything else would have half those rates of failure, the lawsuits would be raining. Where are the flaws, the traps? Love is strong and pure, why is marriage not the reflection of that? All hard to ask questions with little or no answers. Dr. Bak is sharing his reflections and findings as he reached himself the WALL OF MARRIAGE. This is a matter that affects all of our lives. It is time for some answers.

RELEVANCY - TOME TWO -064
REINVENTING OURSELVES TO SURVIVE
BY Dr. BAK NGUYEN & Dr. PAUL OUELLETTE AND COLLABORATORS

THE GREAT PAUSE was a reboot of all the systems of society. Many outdated systems will not make it back. The Dental Industry is a needed one, it has laid on complacency for far too long. In an age where expertise is global and democratized and can be replaced with technologies and artificial intelligence, the REBOOT will force, not just an update, but an operating system replacement and a firmware upgrade. First, they saved their industry with THE ALPHAS INITIATIVE, sharing their knowledge and vision freely to all the world's dental industry. With the OUELLETTE INITIATIVE, they bought some time to all the dental clinics to resume and to adjust. The warning has been given, the clock is now ticking. who will prevail and prosper and who will be left behind, outdated and obsolete?

RISING -062
TO WIN MORE THAN YOU ARE AFRAID TO LOSE
BY Dr. BAK NGUYEN

In RISING, TO WIN MORE TAN YOU ARE AFRAID TO LOSE, Dr. Bak is breaking down the strategy to success to all, not only those wearing white coats and scrubs. More than his previous book (SUCCESS IS A CHOICE), this one is covering most of the aspects of getting to the next level, psychologically, socially, and financially. Rising is broken down into three key strategies: Financial Leverage - Compressing time - Always being in control. Presented by MILLION DOLLAR MINDSET, the book is covering more than the ways to create wealth, but also how to reach happiness and to live a life without regrets. Dr. Bak the CEO and founder of Mdex & Co, a company with the promise of reforming the whole dental industry for the better. He wrote more than 60 books within 30 months as he is sharing his experiences, secrets, and wisdom.

S

SELFMADE -036
GRATITUDE AND HUMILITY
BY Dr. BAK NGUYEN

This is the story of Dr. Bak, an artist who became a dentist, a dentist who became an Entrepreneur, an Entrepreneur who is seeking to save an entire industry. In his free time, Dr. Bak managed to write 37 books and is a contender to 3 world records to be confirmed. Businessman and visionary, his views and philosophy are ahead of our time. This is his 37th book. In SELFMADE, Dr. Bak is answering the questions most entrepreneurs want to know, the HOWTO and the secret recipes, not just to succeed, but to keep going no matter what! SELFMADE is the perfect read for any entrepreneurs, novices, and veterans.

SHORTCUT vol. 1 - HEALING -093
BY Dr. BAK NGUYEN

In SHORTCUT 408 HEALING QUOTES, Dr. Bak revisits and compiles his journey of healing and growing. Just anyone, he was molded and shaped by Conformity and Society to the point of blending and melting. Walking his journey of healing, he rediscovers himself and found his true calling. And once whole with himself and with the Universe, Dr. Bak found his powers. In SHORTCUT 408 HEALING QUOTES, you have a quick and easy way to surf his mindsets and what allowed him to heal, to find back his voice and wings, and to walk his destiny. You too are walking your Quest of Identity. That one is mainly a journey of healing. May you find yours and your powers.

SHORTCUT vol. 2 - GROWING -094
BY Dr. BAK NGUYEN

In SHORTCUT 408 GROWTH QUOTES, Dr. Bak is compiling his library of books about personal growth and self-improvement. More than a motivational book, more than a compilation of knowledge, Dr. Bak is sharing the mindsets upon which he found his power to achieve and to overachieve. We all have our powers, only they were muted and forgotten as we were forged by Conformity and Society. After the healing process, walking your Quest of Identity, the Quest for you growth and God given power is next to lead you to walk your Destiny.

SHORTCUT vol. 3 - LEADERSHIP -095
BY Dr. BAK NGUYEN

In SHORTCUT 365 LEADERSHIP QUOTES, Dr. Bak is compiling his library of books about leadership and ambition. Yes, the ambition is to find your worth and to make the world a better place for all of us. If the 3rd volume of SHORTCUT is mainly a motivational compilation, it also holds the secrets and mindsets to influence and leadership. If you were looking to walk your legend and to impact the world, you are walking a lonely path. You might on your own, but it does not have to be harder than it is. As we all have your unique challenges, the key to victory is often found in the same place, your heart. And here are 365 shortcuts to keep you believing and to attract more people to you as you are growing into a true leader.

SHORTCUT vol. 4 - CONFIDENCE -096
BY Dr. BAK NGUYEN

SHORTCUT 518 CONFIDENCE QUOTES, is the most voluminous compilation of Dr. Bak's quotes. To heal was the first step. To grow and find your powers came next. As you are walking your personal legend, Confidence is both your sword and armour to conquer your Destiny and to overcome all of the challenges on your way. In SHORTCUT volume four, Dr. Bak comprises all his mindsets and wisdom to ease your ascension. Confidence is not something one is simply born with, but something to nurture, grow, and master. Some will have the chance to be raised by people empowering Confidence, others will have to heal from Conformity to grow their confidence. It does not matter, only once Confident, can one stand tall and see clearly the horizon.

SHORTCUT vol. 5- SUCCESS -097
BY Dr. BAK NGUYEN

Success is not a destination but a journey and a side effect. While no map can lead you to success, the right mindset will forge your own success, the one without medals nor labels. If you are looking to walk your legend, to be successful is merely the beginning. Actually, being successful is often a side effect of the mindsets and actions that you took, you provoked. In SHORTCUT 317 SUCCESS QUOTES, Dr. Bak is revisiting his journey, breaking down what led him to be successful despite the odds stacked against him. As success is the consequence of mindsets, choices, and actions, it can be duplicated over and over again, one just needs to master the mindsets first.

SHORTCUT vol. 6- POWER -098
BY Dr. BAK NGUYEN

That's the kind of power that you will discover within this journey. Power is a tool, a leverage. Well used, it will lead to great achievements. Misused, it will be your downfall. If a sword sometimes has 2 edges, Power is a sword with no handle and multiple edges. You have been warned. In SHORTCUT 376 POWER QUOTES, Dr. Bak is compiling all the powers he found and mastered walking his own legend. If the first power was Confidence, very quickly, Dr. Bak realized that Confidence was the key to many, many more powers. Where to find them, how to yield them, and how to leverage these powers is the essence of the 6th volume of SHORTCUT.

SHORTCUT vol. 7- HAPPINESS -099
BY Dr. BAK NGUYEN

We were all born happy and then, somehow, we lost our ways and forgot our ways home. Is this the real tragedy behind the lost paradise myth? If we were happy once, we can trust our heart to find our way home, once more. This is the journey of the 7th volume of the SHORTCUT series. In SHORTCUT 306 HAPPINESS QUOTES, Dr. Bak is revisiting and compiling all the secrets and mindsets leading to happiness. Happiness is not just a destination but a shrine for Confidence and a safe place to regroup, to heal, to grow. We each have our own happiness. What you will learn here is where to find yours and, more importantly, how to leverage you to ease the journey ahead, because happiness is not your final destination. It can be the key to your legend.

SHORTCUT vol. 8- DOCTORS -100
BY Dr. BAK NGUYEN

If healing was the first step to your destiny and powers, there is a science to heal. Those with that science are doctors, the healers of the world. In India, healers are second only to the Gods! In SHORTCUT 170 DOCTOR QUOTES, Dr. Bak is dedicating the 8th volume of the series to his peers, doctors, from all around the world. Doctors too, have to walk their Quest of Identity, to heal from their pain and to walk their legend. Doctors need to heal and rejuvenate to keep healing the world. If healing is their science, in SHORTCUT, they will access the power of leveraging.

SUCCESS IS A CHOICE -060
BLUEPRINTS FOR HEALTH PROFESSIONALS
BY Dr. BAK NGUYEN

In SUCCESS IS A CHOICE, FINANCIAL MILLIONAIRE BLUEPRINTS FOR HEALTH PROFESSIONALS, Dr. Bak is breaking down the strategy to success for all those wearing white coats and scrubs: doctors, dentists, pharmacists, chiropractors, nurses, etc. Success is broken down into three key strategies: Financial Leverage - Compressing time - Always being in control. Presented by MILLION DOLLAR MINDSET, the book is covering more than the ways to create wealth, but also how to reach happiness and to live a life without regrets.Dr. Bak is a successful cosmetic dentist with nearly 20 years of experience. He founded Mdex & Co, a company with the promise of reforming the whole dental industry for the better. While doing so, he discovered a passion for writing and for sharing. Multiple times World Record, Dr. Bak is writing a book every 2 weeks for the last 30 months. This is his 60th book, and he is still practicing. How he does it, is what he is sharing with us, SUCCESS, HAPPINESS, and mostly FREEDOM to all Health Professionals.

SYMPHONY OF SKILLS -001
BY Dr. BAK NGUYEN

You will enlighten the world with your potential. I can't wait to see all the differences that you will have in our world. Remember that power comes with responsibility. We can feel in his presence, a genuine force, a depth of energy, confidence, innocence, courage, and intelligence. Bak is always looking for answers, morning and night, he wants to understand the why and the why not. This book is the essence of the man. Dr. Bak is a force of nature who bears proudly his title eHappy. The man never ceases smiling nor spreading his good vibe wherever he passes. He is not trapped in the nostalgia of the past nor the satisfaction of the present, he embodies the joy of what's possible, what's to come. The more we read, the more we share, and we live. That is Bak, he charms us to evolve and to share his points of view, and before we know it, we are walking by his side, a journey we never saw coming.

T

THE 90 DAYS CHALLENGE -061
BY Dr. BAK NGUYEN

THE 90 DAYS CHALLENGE, is Dr. Bak's journey into the unknown. Overachiever writing 2 books a month on average, for the last 30 months, ambitious CEO, Industries' Disruptor, Dr. Bak seems to have success in everything he touches. Everything except the control of his weight. For nearly 20 years, he struggles with an overweight problem. Every time he scored big, he added on a little more weight. Well, this time, he exposes himself out there, in real-time and without filter, accepting the challenge of his brother-in-law, DON VO to lose 45 pounds within 90 days. That's half a pound a day, for three months. He will have to do so while keeping all of his other challenges on track, writing books at a world record pace, leading the dental industry into the new ERA, and keep seeing his patients. Undoubtedly entertaining, this is the journey of an ALPHA who simply won't give up. But this time, nothing is sure.

THE BOOK OF LEGENDS -024
BY Dr. BAK NGUYEN & WILLIAM BAK

The Book of Legends vol. 1 the story behind the world record of Dr. Bak and his son, William Bak. All Dr. Bak had in mind was to keep his promise of writing a book with his son. They ended up writing 8 children's books within a month, scoring a new world record. William is also the youngest author having published in two languages. Those are world records waiting to be confirmed. History will say: to celebrate a first world record (writing 15 books / 15 months), for the love of his son, he will have scored a second world record: to write 8 books within a month! THE BOOK OF LEGENDS vol. 1 This is both a magical journey for both a father and a son looking to connect and to find themselves. Join Dr. Bak and William Bak in their journey and their love for Life!

THE BOOK OF LEGENDS 2 -041
BY Dr. BAK NGUYEN & WILLIAM BAK

THE BOOK OF LEGENDS vol. 2 is the sequel of "CINDERELLA" but a true story between a father and his son. Together they have discovered a bond and a way to connect. The first BOOK OF LEGENDS covered the time of the first four books they wrote together within a month. The second BOOK OF LEGENDS is covering what happened after the curtains dropped, what happened after reality kicked back in. If the first volume was about a fairy tale in vacation time, the second volume is about making it last in real Life. Share their journey and their love of Life!

THE BOOK OF LEGENDS 3 -086
THE END OF THE INNOCENCE AGE
BY Dr. BAK NGUYEN & WILLIAM BAK

THE BOOK OF LEGENDS 3 is a long work extending on almost 3 years. If the shocking duo known as Dr. Bak and prodigy William Bak has marked the imaginary writing world record upon world record, the story is not all pink. After the franchise of the CHICKEN BOOKS, William, now in his pre-teen years, wants to move away from the chicken tales. After 22 chicken books, a break is well deserved. that said, what is next? Both father and son thought that if they could do it once easily, they could do it again! They couldn't be any further from the truth. For 2 years, they were stuck in the quest for their next franchise of books. THE BOOK OF LEGENDS 3 started right around the end of the chicken franchise and would have ended with a failure if the book was to be released on time, holiday season of that year. It took the duo another year to complete their story to add the last chapters of this book, hoping to end with a happy ending. Unfortunately, not all story ends the way we wish... this is the dark tome of the series, where the imagination got eclipsed. Follow william and dr. bak in they fight to keep the magic and connection alive.

THE CONFESSION OF A LAZY OVERACHIEVER -089
REINVENT YOURSELF FROM ANY CRISIS
BY Dr. BAK NGUYEN

In THE CONFESSION OF A LAZY OVERACHIEVER, Dr. Bak is opening up to his new marketing officer, Jamie, fresh out of school. She is young, full of energy, and looking to chill and still to have it all. True to his character, Dr. Bak is giving Jamie some leeway to redefine Dr. Bak's brand to her demographic, the Millennials. This journey is about Dr. Bak satisfying the Millennials and answering their true questions in life. A rebel himself, his ambition to change the world started back on campus, some 25 years ago... then, life caught up with him. It took Dr. Bak 20 years to shake down the burdens of life, to spread his wings free from Conformity, and to start Overachieving. Doctor, CEO, and world record author, here is what Dr. Bak would have love to know 25 years ago as was still on campus. In a word, this is cheating your way to success and freedom.

And yes, it is possible. Success, Money, Freedom, it all starts with a mindset and the awareness of Time. Welcome to the Alphas.

THE ENERGY FORMULA -053
BY Dr. BAK NGUYEN

THE ENERGY FORMULA is a book dedicated to help each individual to find the means to reach their purpose and goal in Life. Dr. Bak is a philosopher, a strategist, a business, an artist, and a dentist, how does he do all of that? He is doing so while mentoring proteges and leading the modernization of an entire industry. Until now, Momentum and Speed were the powers that he was building on and from. But those powers come from somewhere too. From a guide of our Quest of Identity, he became an ally in everyone's journey for happiness. THE ENERGY FORMULA is the book revealing step by step, the logic of building the right mindset and the way to ABUNDANCE and HAPPINESS, universally. It is not just a HOW TO book, but one that will change your life and guide you to the path of ABUNDANCE.

THE MODERN WOMAN -070
TO HAVE IT HAVE WITH NO SACRIFICE
BY Dr. BAK NGUYEN & Dr. EMILY LETRAN

In THE MODERN WOMAN: TO HAVE IT ALL WITH NO SACRIFICE, Dr. Bak joins forces with Dr. Emily Letran to empower all women to fulfill their desires, goals, and ambition. Both overachievers going against the odds, they are sharing their experience and wisdom to help all women to find confidence and support to redefine their lives. Dr. Emily Letran is a doctor in dentistry, an entrepreneur, author, and CERTIFIED HIGH-PERFORMANCE coach. For an Asian woman, she made it through the norms and the red tapes to find her voice. As she learned and grew with mentors, today she is sharing her secret with the energy that will motivate all of the female genders to stand for what they deserve. Alpha doctor, Bak is joining his voice and perspective since this is not about gender equality, but about personal empowerment and the quest of Identity of each, man and woman. Once more, Dr. Bak is bringing LEVERAGE and REASON to the new social deal between man and woman. This is not about gender, but about confidence.

THE POWER BEHIND THE ALPHA -008
BY TRANIE VO & Dr. BAK NGUYEN

It's been said by a "great man" that "We are born alone and we die alone." Both men and women proudly repeat those words as wisdom since. I apologize in advance, but what a fat LIE! That's what I learned and discovered in life since my mind and heart got liberated from the burden of scars and the ladders of society. I can have it all, not all at the same time, but I can have everything I put my mind and heart into. Actually, it is not completely true. I can have most of what I and Tranie put our minds into. Together, when we feel like one, there isn't much out of our reach. If I'm the mind, she's the heart; if I'm the Will, she's the means. Synergy is the core of our power. Tranie's aim is always Happiness. In Tranie's definition of life, there are no justifications, no excuses, no tomorrow. For Tranie, Happiness is measured by the minutes of every single day. This is why she's so strong and can heal people around her. That may also be why she doesn't need to talk much, since talking about the past or the future is, in her mind, dimming down the magic of the present, the Now. We both respect and appreciate that we are the whole balancing each other's equation of life, of love, of success. I was the plus and the minus, then I became the multiplication factor and grew into the exponential. And how is Tranie evolving in all of this? She is and always will be the balance. If anything, she is the equal sign of each equation.

THE POWER OF Dr. -066
THE MODERN TITLE OF NOBILITY
BY Dr. BAK NGUYEN, Dr. PAVEL KRASTEV AND COLLABORATORS

In THE POWER OF Dr., independent thinkers mean to exchange ideas. An idea can be very powerful if supported with a great work ethic. Work ethic, isn't that the main fabric of our white coats, scrubs, and title? In an era post-COVID where everything has been rebooted and that the healthcare industry is facing its own fate: to evolve or to be replaced, Dr. Bak and Dr. Pavel reveal the source of their power and their playbook to move forward, ahead. The power we all hold is our resilience and discipline. We put that for years at the service of our profession, from a surgical perspective. Now, we can harness that same power to rewrite the rules, the industry, and our future. Post-COVID, the rules are being rewritten, will you be part of the team or left behind? "You can be in control!" More than personal growth and a motivational book, THE POWER OF Dr. is an awakening call to the doctor you look at when you graduate, with hope, with honour, with determination.

THE POWER OF YES -010
VOLUME ONE: IMPACT
BY Dr. BAK NGUYEN

In THE POWER OF YES, Dr. Bak is sharing his journey opening up and embracing the world, one day at a time, one ask at a time, one wish at a time. Far from a dare, saying YES allowed Dr. Bak to rewrite his mindsets and to break all the boundaries. This book is not one written a few days or weeks, but the accumulation of a journey for 12 months. The journeys started as Dr. Bak said YES to his producer to go on stage and to speak... That YES opened a world of possibilities. Dr. Bak embraced each and every one of them. 12 months later, he is celebrating the new world record of writing 9 books written over a period of 12 months. To him, it will be a miss, missing the 12 on 12 mark. To the rest of the world, they just saw the birth of a force of nature, the Alpha force. THE POWER OF YES is comprised of all the introduction of the adult books written by Dr. Bak within the first 12 months. Chapter by chapter, you can walk in his footstep seeing and smelling what he has. This is reality literature with a twist of POWER. THE POWER OF YES! Discover your potential and your power. This is the POWER OF YES, volume one. Welcome to the Alphas.

THE POWER OF YES 2 -037
VOLUME TWO: SHAPELESS
BY Dr. BAK NGUYEN

In THE POWER OF YES, volume 2, Dr. Bak is continuing his journey discovering his powers and influence. After 12 months embracing the world saying YES, he rose as an emerging force: he's been recognized as an INDUSTRIES DISRUPTOR, got nominated ERNST AND YOUNG ENTREPRENEUR OF THE YEAR, wrote 9 books within 12 months while launching the most ambitious private endeavour to reform his own industry, the dental field. Contender too many WORLD RECORDS, Dr. Bak is doing all of that in parallel. And yes, he is sleeping his nights and yes, he is writing his book himself, from the screen of his iPhone! Far from satisfied, Dr. Bak missed the mark of writing 12 books within 12 months and everything else is shaping and moving, and could come crumbling down at each turn. Now that Dr. Bak understands his powers, he is looking to test them and to push them to their limits, looking to keep scoring world records while materializing his vision and enterprises. This is the awakening of a Force of Nature looking to change the world for the better while having fun sharing. Welcome to the Alphas.

THE POWER OF YES 3 -046
VOLUME THREE: LIMITLESS
BY Dr. BAK NGUYEN

In THE POWER OF YES, volume 3, the journey of Dr. Bak continues where the last volume left, in front of 300 plus people showing up to his first solo event, a Dr. Bak's event. On stage and in this book, Dr. Bak reveals how 12 months saying YES to everything changed his life… actually, it was 18 months. From a dentist looking to change the world from a dental chair into a multiple times world record author, the journey of openness is a rendez-vous with Fate. Dr. Bak is sharing almost in real-time his journey, experiences, but above all, his feelings, doubts, and comebacks. From one book to the next, from one journey to the next, follow the adventure of a man looking to find his name, his worth, and his place in the world. Doing so, he is touching people Doing so, he is touching people and initiating their rises. Are you ready for more? Are you ready to meet your Fate and Destiny? Welcome to the Alphas.

THE POWER OF YES 4 -087
VOLUME FOUR: PURPOSE
BY Dr. BAK NGUYEN

In THE POWER OF YES, volume 4, the journey continues days after where the last volume left. After setting the new world record of writing 48 books within 24 months, Dr. Bak is not ready to stop. As volume one covers 12 months of journey, volume 2 covers 6 months. Well, volume 3 covers 4 months. The speed is building up and increasing, steadily. This is volume 4, RISING, after breaking the sound barrier. Dr. Bak has reached a state where he is above most resistance and friction, he is now in a universe of his own, discovering his powers as he walks his journeys. This is no fiction story or wishful thinking, THE POWER OF YES is the journey of Dr. Bak, from one world record to the next, from one book to the next. You too can walk your own legend, you just need to listen to your innersole and to open up to the opportunity. May you get inspiration from the legendary journey of Dr. Bak and find your own Destiny. Welcome to the Alphas.

THE RISE OF THE UNICORN -038
BY Dr. BAK NGUYEN & Dr. JEAN DE SERRES

In THE RISE OF THE UNICORN, Dr. Bak is joining forces with his friend and mentor, Dr. Jean De Serres. Together both men had many achievements in their respective industries, but the advent of eHappyPedia, THE RISE OF THE UNICORN is a personal project dear to both of them: the QUEST OF HAPPINESS and its empowerment. This book is a special one since you are witnessing the conversation between two entrepreneurs looking to change the world by building unique tools and media. Just like any enterprise, the ride is never a smooth one in the park on a beautiful day. But this is about eHappyPedia, it is about happiness, right? So it will happen and with a smile attached to it! The unique value of this book is that you are sharing the ups and downs of the launch of a Unicorn, not just the glory of the fame, but also the doubts and challenges on the way. May it inspire you on your own journey to success and happiness.

THE RISE OF THE UNICORN 2 -076
eHappyPedia
BY Dr. BAK NGUYEN & Dr. JEAN DE SERRES

This is 2 years after starting the first tome. Dr. Bak's brand is picking up, between the accumulation of records and the recognition. eHappyPedia is now hot for a comeback. In THE RISE OF THE UNICORN 2, Dr. Bak is retracing and addressing each of Dr. Jean De Serres' concerns about the weakness of the first version of eHappyPedia and the eHappy movement. This is the sort of the creation and a UNICORN both in finance and in psychology. Never before, you will assist in such daily and decision-making process of a world phenomenon and of a company. Dr. Bak and Dr. De Serres are literally using the process of writing this series of books to plan and to brainstorm the birth of a bluechip. More than an intriguing story, this is the journey of 2 experienced entrepreneurs changing the world.

THE U.A.X STORY -072
THE ULTIMATE AUDIO EXPERIENCE
BY Dr. BAK NGUYEN

This is the story of the ULTIMATE AUDIO EXPERIENCE, U.A.X. Follow Dr. Bak's footstep on how he invented a new way to read and to learn. Dr. Bak brings his experience as a movie producer and a director to elevate the reading experience to another level with entertaining value and make it accessible to everyone, auditive, and visual people alike. Three years plus of research and development, countless hours of trials and errors, Dr. Bak finally solved his puzzle: having written more than 1.1 million words. The irony is that he does not like to read, he likes audiobooks! U.A.X. finally allowed the opening of Dr. Bak's entire library to a new genre and media. U.A.X. is the new way to learn and enjoy Audiobooks. Made to be entertaining while keeping the self-educational value of a book, U.A.X. will appeal to both auditive and visual people. U.A.X. is the blockbuster of the Audiobooks. The format has already been approved by iTunes, Amazon, Spotify, and all major platforms for global distribution and streaming.

THE VACCINE -077
BY Dr. BAK NGUYEN & WILLIAM BAK

In THE VACCINE, A TALE OF SPIES AND ALIENS, Dr. Bak reprise his role as mentor to William, his 10 years-old son, both as co-author and as doctor. William is living through the COVID war and has accumulated many, many questions. That morning, they got out all at once. From a conversation between father and son, Dr. Bak is making science into words keeping the interest of his son a Saturday morning in bed. William is not just an audience, he is responsible to map the field with his questions. What started as a morning conversation between father and son, became within the next hour, a great project, their 23rd book together. Learn about the virus, vaccination while entertaining your kids.

TIMING - TIME MANAGEMENT ON STEROIDS -074
BY Dr. BAK NGUYEN & WILLIAM BAK

In TIMING, TIME MANAGEMENT ON STEROIDS, Dr. Bak is sharing his secret to keep overachieving, overdelivering while raising the bar higher and higher. We all have 24 hours in a day, so how can some do so much more than others. Dr. Bak is not only sharing his secrets and mindset about time and efficiency, he is literally living his own words as this book is written within his last sprint to set the next world record of writing 100 books within 4 years, with only 31 days to go. With 8 books to write in 31 days, that's a little less than 4 days per book! Share the journey of a man surfing the change and looking to see where is the limit of the human mind, writing. In the meantime, understand his leverage, mindset, and secrets to challenge your own limits and dreams.

TO OVERACHIEVE EVERYTHING BEING LAZY -090
CHEAT YOUR WAY TO SUCCESS
BY Dr. BAK NGUYEN

In TO OVERACHIEVE EVERYTHING BEING LAZY, Dr. Bak retaking his role talking to the millennials, the next generation. If in the first tome of the series LAZY, Dr. Bak addresses the general audience of millennials, especially young women, he is dedicating this tome to the ALPHA amongst the millennials, those aiming for the moon and looking, not only to be happy but to change the world. This is not another take on how to cheat your way to success or how to leverage laziness, but this is the recipe to build overachievers and rainmakers. For the young leaders with ambitions and talent, understanding TIME and ENERGY are crucial from your first steps writing your our legend. If Dr. Bak had the chance to do it all over again, this is how he would do it! Welcome to the Alphas.

TORNADO -067
FORCE OF CHANGE
BY Dr. BAK NGUYEN

In TORNADO - FORCE OF CHANGE Dr. Bak is writing solo. In the midst of the COVID war, change is not a good intention anymore. Change, constant change has become a new reality, a new norm. From somebody who holds the title of Industries' Disruptor, how does he yield change to stay in control? Well, the changes from the COVID war are constant fear and much loss of individual liberty. Some can endure the change, some will ride it. Dr. Bak is sharing his angle of navigating the changes, yielding the improvisations, and to reinvent the goals, the means to stay relevant. From fighting to keep his companies Dr. Bak went on to let go the uncontrollable to embrace the opportunity, he reinvented himself to ride the change and create opportunities from an unprecedented crisis. This is the story of a man refusing to kneel and accept defeat, smiling back at faith to find leverage and hope.

TOUCHSTONE -073
LEVERAGING TODAY'S PSYCHOLOGICAL SMOG
BY Dr. BAK NGUYEN & Dr. KEN SEROTA

TOUCHSTONE, LEVERAGING TODAY'S PSYCHOLOGICAL SMOG is mapping to navigate and to thrive in today's high and constant stress environment. After 40 years in practice, Dr. Serota is concerned about the evolution of the career of health care professionals and the never-ending level of stress. What is stress, what are its effects, damages, and symptoms? If COVID-19 revealed to the world that we are fragile, it also revealed most of the broken and the flaws of our system. For now a century, dentistry has been a champion in depression, Drug addiction, and suicide rate, and the curve is far from flattening. Dr. Bak is sharing his perspective and experience dealing with stress and how to leverage it into a constructive force. From the stress of a doctor with no right to failure to the stress of an entrepreneur never knowing the future, Dr. Bak is sharing his way to use stress as leverage.

ABOUT THE AUTHORS

From Canada, **Dr. BAK NGUYEN**, Nominee Ernst and Young Entrepreneur of the year, Grand Homage Lys DIVERSITY, LinkedIn & TownHall Achiever of the year and TOP 100 Doctors 2021. Dr. Bak is a cosmetic dentist, CEO and founder of Mdex & Co. His company is revolutionizing the dental field.

Speaker and motivator, he holds the world record of writing 100 books in 4 years accumulating many world records (to be officialized). Before that he held the world record of writing 9 books over 12 months, then, 15 books within 15 months to set the bar even higher with the world record of 36 books written within 18 months + 1 week.

By his second author anniversary, he scored his new landmark world record of 48 books within 24 months. And then 72 books in 36 months. By the 4th anniversary Dr. Bak scored his usually landmark of writing 96 books over 48 months, but he pushed even further, scoring also the new world record of 100 books written within 4 years!

His books are covering:

- **ENTREPRENEURSHIP**
- **LEADERSHIP**
- **QUEST OF IDENTITY**
- **DENTISTRY AND MEDICINE**
- **PARENTING**
- **CHILDREN BOOKS**
- **PHILOSOPHY**

In 2003, he founded Mdex, a dental company upon which in 2018, he launched the most ambitious private endeavour to reform the dental industry, Canada wide. Philosopher, he has close to his heart the quest of happiness of the people surrounding him, patients and colleagues alike. In 2020, he launched an International collaborative initiative named **THE ALPHAS** to share knowledge and for Entrepreneurs and Doctors to thrive through the Greatest Pandemic and Economic depression of our time.

In 2016, he co-found with Tranie Vo, Emotive World Incorporated, a tech research company to use technology to empower happiness and sharing. U.A.X. the ultimate audio experience is the landmark project on which the team is advancing, utilizing the technics of the movie industry and the advancement in ARTIFICIAL INTELLIGENCE to save the book industry and to upgrade the continuing education space.

These projects have allowed Dr. Nguyen to attract interests from the international and diplomatic community and he is now the centre of a global discussion in the wellbeing and the future of the health profession. It is in that matter that he shares his thoughts and encourages the health community to share their own stories.

> "It's not worth it go through it alone! Together, we stand, alone, we fall."

Motivational speaker and serial entrepreneur, philosopher and author, from his own words, Dr. Nguyen describes himself as a dentist by circumstances, an entrepreneur by nature and a communicator by passion.

He also holds recognitions from the Canadian Parliament and the Canadian Senate.

From Canada, **William Bak**, is an 12 years old prodigy. At the age of 8 years old, he co-wrote a series of chicken books with his dad, Dr. Bak. Together, they are changing the world, one mind at a time, writing books for kids. So far, they have 32 books together.

He co-wrote the 11 chicken books in ENGLISH and then, had to translate his own books in FRENCH. This is how he has 22 chicken books. William also co-wrote 2 parenting books with his dad, Dr. Bak, THE BOOK OF LEGENDS volumes 1, 2 and 3; the first volume of THE RISE OF LEGENDS; 2 Vaccine books (French and English); TIMING, William first Apollo Protocol book. Lately, William has also wrote his first book solo at the age of 11, PAPA, J'SUIS PAS CON and the PROLOGUES OF DESTINY, volume 1 and 2, and AU PAYS DES PAPAS 1 and 2.

To promote his books, William embraced the stage for the first time in 2019 talking to a crowd of 300+ people. Since, he has appeared in many videos to talk about his books and upcoming projects.

In the midst of COVID, he got bored and started his YOUTUBE CHANNEL : GAMEBAK, reviewing video games.
By the end of 2020, he has joined THE ALPHAS as the youngest anchor of the upcoming world project COVIDCONOMICS in which he will give his perspective and host the opinions of his generation.

"I will show you. I won't force you. But I won't wait for you."
- William Bak and Dr. Bak

Writing with his Dad, William holds world records to be officialized:

- The youngest author writing in 2 languages
- Co-author of 8 books within a month
- The first kid to have written 20 children books
- The child to have written his first solo book in 9 days
- The first child who wrote 33 books within 43 months

ULTIMATE AUDIO EXPERIENCE

A new way to learn and enjoy Audiobooks. Made to be entertaining while keeping the self-educational value of a book, UAX will appeal to both auditive and visual people. UAX is the blockbuster of the Audiobooks.

UAX will cover most of Dr Bak's books, and is now negotiating to bring more authors and more titles to the UAX concept. Now streaming on Spotify, Apple Music and available for download on all major music platforms. Give it a try today!

AMAZON - BARNES & NOBLE - APPLE BOOKS - KINDLE
SPOTIFY - APPLE MUSIC

COMBO
PAPERBACK/AUDIOBOOK
ACTIVATION

Please register your book to receive the link to your audiobook version. Register at: https://baknguyen.com/rise-of-legends-registry

Your license of the audiobook allows you to share with up to 3 peoples the audiobook contained at this link. Book published by Dr. Bak publishing company. Audiobook produced by Emotive World Inc. Copyright 2021, All right reserved.

FROM THE SAME AUTHOR
Dr. Bak Nguyen

TITLES AVAILABLE at
www.Dr.BakNguyen.com

MAJOR LEAGUES' ACCESS

FACTEUR HUMAIN -035
LE LEADERSHIP DU SUCCÈS
par Dr. BAK NGUYEN & CHRISTIAN TRUDEAU

THE RISE OF THE UNICORN -038
BY Dr. BAK NGUYEN & Dr. JEAN DE SERRES

CHAMPION MINDSET -039
LEARNING TO WIN
BY Dr. BAK NGUYEN & CHRISTOPHE MULUMBA

THE RISE OF THE UNICORN 2 -076
eHappyPedia
BY Dr. BAK NGUYEN & Dr. JEAN DE SERRES

BRANDING -044
BALANCING STRATEGY AND EMOTIONS
BY Dr. BAK NGUYEN

BUSINESS

SYMPHONY OF SKILLS -001
BY Dr. BAK NGUYEN

LA SYMPHONIE DES SENS -002
ENTREPREUNARIAT
par Dr. BAK NGUYEN

INDUSTRIES DISRUPTORS -006
BY Dr. BAK NGUYEN

CHANGING THE WORLD FROM A DENTAL CHAIR -007
BY Dr. BAK NGUYEN

THE POWER BEHIND THE ALPHA -008
BY TRANIE VO & Dr. BAK NGUYEN

SELFMADE -036
GRATITUDE AND HUMILITY
BY Dr. BAK NGUYEN

THE U.A.X STORY -072
THE ULTIMATE AUDIO EXPERIENCE
BY Dr. BAK NGUYEN

CRYPTOCONOMICS 101 - TO COME
MY PERSONAL JOURNEY FROM 50K TO 1 MILLION
BY Dr. BAK NGUYEN

CHILDREN'S BOOK
with William Bak

The Trilogy of Legends

THE LEGEND OF THE CHICKEN HEART -016
LA LÉGENDE DU COEUR DE POULET -017
BY Dr. BAK NGUYEN & WILLIAM BAK

THE LEGEND OF THE LION HEART -018
LA LÉGENDE DU COEUR DE LION -019
BY Dr. BAK NGUYEN & WILLIAM BAK

THE LEGEND OF THE DRAGON HEART -020
LA LÉGENDE DU COEUR DE Dr.AGON -021
BY Dr. BAK NGUYEN & WILLIAM BAK

WE ARE ALL DRAGONS -022
NOUS TOUS, DRAGONS -023
BY Dr. BAK NGUYEN & WILLIAM BAK

THE 9 SECRETS OF THE SMART CHICKEN -025
LES 9 SECRETS DU POULET INTELLIGENT -026
BY Dr. BAK NGUYEN & WILLIAM BAK

THE SECRET OF THE FAST CHICKEN -027
LE SECRETS DU POULET RAPIDE -028
BY Dr. BAK NGUYEN & WILLIAM BAK

THE LEGEND OF THE SUPER CHICKEN -029
LA LÉGENDE DU SUPER POULET -030
BY Dr. BAK NGUYEN & WILLIAM BAK

THE STORY OF THE CHICKEN SHIT -031
L'HISTOIRE DU CACA DE POULET -032
BY Dr. BAK NGUYEN & WILLIAM BAK

WHY CHICKEN CAN'T DREAM? -033
POURQUOI LES POULETS NE RÊVENT PAS? -034
BY Dr. BAK NGUYEN & WILLIAM BAK

THE STORY OF THE CHICKEN NUGGET -057
HISTOIRE DE POULET: LA PÉPITE -083
BY Dr. BAK NGUYEN & WILLIAM BAK

CHICKEN FOREVER -082
POULET POUR TOUJOURS -084
BY Dr. BAK NGUYEN & WILLIAM BAK

THE SPIES AND ALIENS COLLECTION

THE VACCINE -077
LE VACCIN -079
LA VACUNA -077B
BY Dr. BAK NGUYEN & WILLIAM BAK
TRANSLATION BY BRENDA GARCIA

DENTISTRY

PROFESSION HEALTH - TOME ONE -005
THE UNCONVENTIONAL QUEST OF HAPPINESS
BY Dr. BAK NGUYEN, Dr. MIRJANA SINDOLIC,
Dr. ROBERT DURAND AND COLLABORATORS

HOW TO NOT FAIL AS A DENTIST -047
BY Dr. BAK NGUYEN

SUCCESS IS A CHOICE -060
BLUEPRINTS FOR HEALTH PROFESSIONALS
BY Dr. BAK NGUYEN

RELEVANCY - TOME TWO -064
REINVENTING OURSELVES TO SURVIVE
BY Dr. BAK NGUYEN & Dr. PAUL OUELLETTE AND COLLABORATORS

MIDAS TOUCH -065
POST-COVID DENTISTRY
BY Dr. BAK NGUYEN, Dr. JULIO REYNAFARJE AND Dr. PAUL OUELLETTE

THE POWER OF Dr. -066
THE MODERN TITLE OF NOBILITY
BY Dr. BAK NGUYEN, Dr. PAVEL KRASTEV AND COLLABORATORS

ALPHA DENTISTRY vol. 1 -104
DIGITAL ORTHODONTICS FAQ
BY Dr. BAK NGUYEN

ALPHA DENTISTRY vol. 1 -109
DIGITAL ORTHODONTICS FAQ ASSEMBLED EDITION
USA SPAIN GERMANY INDIA CANADA
BY Dr. BAK NGUYEN, Dr. PAUL OUELLETTE, Dr. PAUL DOMINIQUE, Dr. MARIA KUNSTADTER, Dr. EDWARD J. ZUCKERBERG, Dr. MASHA KHAGHANI, Dr. SUJATA BASAWARAJ, Dr. ALVA AURORA, Dr. JUDITH BÄUMLER, and Dr. ASHISH GUPTA

ALPHA DENTISTRY vol. 1 -113
DIGITAL ORTHODONTICS FAQ INTERNATIONAL EDITION
🇺🇸 ENGLISH 🇦🇷 SPANISH 🇩🇪 GERMAN 🇮🇳 HINDI 🇨🇦 FRENCH
BY Dr. BAK NGUYEN, Dr. PAUL OUELLETTE, Dr. PAUL DOMINIQUE, Dr. MARIA KUNSTADTER, Dr. EDWARD J. ZUCKERBERG, Dr. MASHA KHAGHANI, Dr. SUJATA BASAWARAJ, Dr. ALVA AURORA, Dr. JUDITH BÄUMLER, and Dr. ASHISH GUPTA

KISS ORTHODONTICS -105
BY Dr. BAK NGUYEN, Dr. PAUL OUELLETTE
WITH GUEST AUTHORS Dr. RYAN HUNGATE and Dr. MAHSA KHAGHANI

QUEST OF IDENTITY

IDENTITY -004
THE ANTHOLOGY OF QUESTS
BY Dr. BAK NGUYEN

HYBRID -011
THE MODERN QUEST OF IDENTITY
BY Dr. BAK NGUYEN

LIFESTYLE

HORIZON, BUILDING UP THE VISION -045
VOLUME ONE
BY Dr. BAK NGUYEN

HORIZON, ON THE FOOTSTEP OF TITANS -048
VOLUME TWO
BY Dr. BAK NGUYEN

HORIZON, Dr.EAMING OF THE FUTURE -068
VOLUME THREE
BY Dr. BAK NGUYEN

MILLION DOLLAR MINDSET

MOMENTUM TRANSFER -009
BY Dr. BAK NGUYEN & Coach DINO MASSON

LEVERAGE -014
COMMUNICATION INTO SUCCESS
BY Dr. BAK NGUYEN

HOW TO WRITE A BOOK IN 30 DAYS -042
BY Dr. BAK NGUYEN

POWER -043
EMOTIONAL INTELLIGENCE
BY Dr. BAK NGUYEN

HOW TO WRITE A SUCCESSFUL BUSINESS PLAN -049
BY Dr. BAK NGUYEN & ROUBA SAKR

MINDSET ARMORY -050
BY Dr. BAK NGUYEN

MASTERMIND, 7 WAYS INTO THE BIG LEAGUE -052
BY Dr. BAK NGUYEN & JONAS DIOP

PLAYBOOK INTRODUCTION -055
BY Dr. BAK NGUYEN

PLAYBOOK INTRODUCTION 2 -056
BY Dr. BAK NGUYEN

RISING -062
TO WIN MORE THAN YOU ARE AFRAID TO LOSE
BY Dr. BAK NGUYEN

TORNADO -067
FORCE OF CHANGE
BY Dr. BAK NGUYEN

BOOTCAMP -071
**BOOKS TO REWRITE MINDSETS
INTO WINNING STATES OF MIND**
BY Dr. BAK NGUYEN

TIMING -074
TIME MANAGEMENT ON STEROIDS
BY Dr. BAK NGUYEN

POWERPLAY -078
HOW TO BUILD THE PERFECT TEAM
BY Dr. BAK NGUYEN

HOW TO BOOST YOUR CREATIVITY TO NEW HEIGHTS -088
BY Dr. BAK NGUYEN

PARENTING

THE BOOK OF LEGENDS -024
BY Dr. BAK NGUYEN & WILLIAM BAK

THE BOOK OF LEGENDS 2 -041
BY Dr. BAK NGUYEN & WILLIAM BAK

THE BOOK OF LEGENDS 3 -086
THE END OF THE INNOCENCE AGE
BY Dr. BAK NGUYEN & WILLIAM BAK

THE ORIGIN SERIES

L'ART DE TRANSFORMER DE LA SOUPE EN MAGIE -103
PAR Dr. BAK NGUYEN

AU PAYS DES PAPAS -106
PAR Dr. BAK NGUYEN & WILLIAM BAK

AU PAYS DES PAPAS 2 -108
PAR Dr. BAK NGUYEN & WILLIAM BAK

PERSONAL GROWTH

REBOOT -012
MIDLIFE CRISIS
BY Dr. BAK NGUYEN

HUMILITY FOR SUCCESS -051
BALANCING STRATEGY AND EMOTIONS
BY Dr. BAK NGUYEN

THE ENERGY FORMULA -053
BY Dr. BAK NGUYEN

AMONGST THE ALPHAS -058
BY Dr. BAK NGUYEN, with Dr. MARIA KUNSTADTER,
Dr. PAUL OUELLETTE and Dr. JEREMY KRELL

AMONGST THE ALPHAS vol.2 -059
ON THE OTHER SIDE
BY Dr. BAK NGUYEN with Dr. JULIO REYNAFARJE,
Dr. LINA DUSEVICIUTE and Dr. DUC-MINH LAM-DO

THE 90 DAYS CHALLENGE -061
BY Dr. BAK NGUYEN

EMPOWERMENT -069
BY Dr. BAK NGUYEN

THE MODERN WOMAN -070
TO HAVE IT HAVE WITH NO SACRIFICE
BY Dr. BAK NGUYEN & Dr. EMILY LETRAN

ALPHA LADDERS -075
CAPTAIN OF YOUR DESTINY
BY Dr. BAK NGUYEN & JONAS DIOP

1SELF -080
REINVENT YOURSELF FROM ANY CRISIS
BY Dr. BAK NGUYEN

THE LAZY FRANCHISE

THE CONFESSION OF A LAZY OVERACHIEVER -089
REINVENT YOURSELF FROM ANY CRISIS
BY Dr. BAK NGUYEN

TO OVERACHIEVE EVERYTHING BEING LAZY -090
CHEAT YOUR WAY TO SUCCESS
BY Dr. BAK NGUYEN

PHILOSOPHY

LEADERSHIP -003
PANDORA'S BOX
BY Dr. BAK NGUYEN

FORCES OF NATURE -015
FORGING THE CHARACTER OF WINNERS
BY Dr. BAK NGUYEN

ALPHA LADDERS 2 -081
SHAPING LEADERS AND ACHIEVERS
BY Dr. BAK NGUYEN & BRENDA GARCIA

MIRROR -085
BY Dr. BAK NGUYEN

SHORTCUT

408 HEALING QUOTES -093
SHORTCUT VOLUME ONE
BY Dr. BAK NGUYEN

408 GROWTH QUOTES -094
SHORTCUT VOLUME TWO
BY Dr. BAK NGUYEN

365 LEADERSHIP QUOTES -095
SHORTCUT VOLUME THREE
BY Dr. BAK NGUYEN

518 CONFIDENCE QUOTES -096
SHORTCUT VOLUME FOUR

BY Dr. BAK NGUYEN

317 SUCCESS QUOTES -097
SHORTCUT VOLUME FIVE

BY Dr. BAK NGUYEN

376 POWER QUOTES -098
SHORTCUT VOLUME SIX

BY Dr. BAK NGUYEN

306 HAPPINESS QUOTES -099
SHORTCUT VOLUME SEVEN

BY Dr. BAK NGUYEN

170 DOCTOR QUOTES -100
SHORTCUT VOLUME EIGHT

BY Dr. BAK NGUYEN

SOCIETY

LE RÊVE CANADIEN -013
D'IMMIGRANT À MILLIONNAIRE

par Dr. BAK NGUYEN

KRYPTO -040
TO SAVE THE WORLD

BY Dr. BAK NGUYEN & ILYAS BAKOUCH

CHOC -054
LE JARDIN D'EDITH

par Dr. BAK NGUYEN

AFTERMATH -063
BUSINESS AFTER THE GREAT PAUSE
BY Dr. BAK NGUYEN & Dr. ERIC LACOSTE

TOUCHSTONE -073
LEVERAGING TODAY'S PSYCHOLOGICAL SMOG
BY Dr. BAK NGUYEN & Dr. KEN SEROTA

COVIDCONOMICS - TO COME
THE GENERATION AHEAD
BY Dr. BAK NGUYEN

TEEN'S FICTION
with William Bak

LEGENDS OF DESTINY

THE PROLOGUES OF DESTINY -101
VOLUME ONE
BY Dr. BAK NGUYEN & WILLIAM BAK

THE BOOK OF ELVES -107
VOLUME TWO
BY Dr. BAK NGUYEN & WILLIAM BAK

THE POWER OF YES

THE POWER OF YES -010
VOLUME ONE: IMPACT
BY Dr. BAK NGUYEN

THE POWER OF YES 2 -037
VOLUME TWO: SHAPELESS
BY Dr. BAK NGUYEN

THE POWER OF YES 3 -046
VOLUME THREE: LIMITLESS
BY Dr. BAK NGUYEN

THE POWER OF YES 4 -087
VOLUME FOUR: PURPOSE
BY Dr. BAK NGUYEN

THE POWER OF YES 5 -091
VOLUME FIVE: ALPHA
BY Dr. BAK NGUYEN

THE POWER OF YES 6 -092
VOLUME SIX: PERSPECTIVE
BY Dr. BAK NGUYEN

TITLES AVAILABLE AT
www.Dr.BakNguyen.com

AMAZON - APPLE BOOKS - KINDLE - SPOTIFY - APPLE MUSIC

Since Dr. Bak set his new landmark world record writing 100 books in 4 years, he is opening his entire audio library, audiobooks and UAX albums, exclusively to all VIP members for $9.99/month.

Becoming a VIP member, you will have access to all Dr. Bak's audiobooks and UAX albums. Those are the only today bought at Apple Books, Audible, and in COMBO version at Amazon. The UAX albums are those streaming on Apple Music, Spotify, and Amazon Prime Music.

As a VIP, you will also have prime access to the audiobooks as soon as they are completed, hitting them before they reach the mainstream outlets. Get your membership today!

http://drbaknguyen.com/members

Welcome to the Alphas.

www.ingramcontent.com/pod-product-compliance
Lightning Source LLC
Chambersburg PA
CBHW071423150426
43191CB00008B/1027